C000152759

LEAF PLAN

TOWARDS THE ECOLOGICAL TRANSITION

Mosè Ricci

Sara Favargiotti

Content

#Vision

Leaf Plan Trento.
The Existing as the New Heritage

Mosè Ricci

The future city is the one that already exists

During last decades new planning paradigms have been shaping our cities: urban areas have been competing to reposition themselves in the global economic framework, starting the so called "Urban Regeneration" process that lead to the renovation of public space and to the construction of innovative neighborhoods; cities started the implementation of new technological systems, such as transport management systems, water and contamination monitoring systems, smart energy grids and energy efficient buildings, leading to the implementation of the "Smart City"; the demand for new environmental sensitivity in urban planning has led to a new sustainable approach: the words "Regeneration", "Recycling", "Re-Naturalization" and "Recovery" tend to identify the new-urban territorial agendas of the beginning of this century. Even though, thanks to the implementation of these planning paradigms, European cities have strengthened their economy, efficiency and livability, in order to respond to the latest challenges, as defined by the United Nations Sustainable Development Goals (SDG) 2016-30, it is necessary to work on cities with a new holistic approach. At the Habitat III Summit, the New Urban Agenda, in line with the SDG, has been defined and includes the following objectives: providing basic services for all citizens; ensuring that all citizens have access to equal opportunities and face no discrimination; promoting measures that support cleaner cities; strengthening resilience in cities to reduce the risk and the impact of disasters; taking action to address climate change by reducing their greenhouse gas emissions; improving connectivity and support innovative and green initiatives; promoting safe, accessible and green public spaces (UN-Habitat 2018).

Now the simultaneous action of three key factors: the post-pandemic social/economic crisis, the new environmental awareness and the sharing information technologies revolution is so deeply changing our lifestyles and the way we imagine and we want the solid forms of our future that all our design knowledge suddenly seems inadequate both as an interpretative tool of the current habitat conditions and as a device capable of generating new environmental, social, economic performances and new beauty and happiness.

The development model based on the concentration and speed of flows in a metropolitan settlement horizon enters into a strong crisis with the epidemic emergency. Concentration levels of PM10 and PM2.5, as many recent

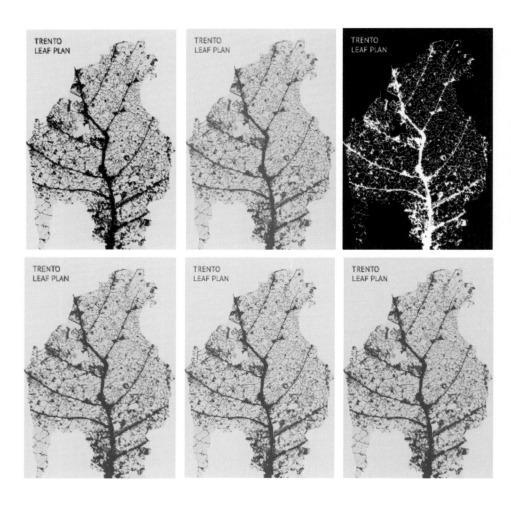

01 | Leaf plan Manifesto

studies seem to demonstrate, lead to the more intense spread of the disease. Right now is the time to affirm a vision no longer degenerative of habitats development – which requires energy and materials to produce goods that will become waste – but regenerative, that is, which recycles energy and materials and which is capable of cultivating human nature and its natural, social and cultural environment.

Richard Sennet speaks of the need for Open Urbanism for an open city of the future, especially after the pandemic. An "open urbanism" to build a flexible environment, not overdetermined or completely defined a priori, so as to preserve the benefits of living together in the cities but avoid the most dangerous threats. Those deriving from viruses and diseases, but also those related to the effects of climate change.

There is a New Urban Heritage that should not be cancelled, but re-generated. In Italy there are at least 8 million empty houses that need to be re-inhabited before building more, and every new land use has unsustainable environmental costs. The city of Trento, which is the largest city in Trentino, contains within it a quantity of unused empty spaces that by total volume would represent the second largest city in Trentino.

The city of the future is mainly the one that already exists because there are millions of empty houses to live in before building others and because every new land consumption has unsustainable environmental costs. The role of design disciplines is no longer to conceive and organise the construction of the new. In a completely changed context (post-modern, post-pandemic, ...) urbanism, landscape, architecture and design can finally return to taking care of people and their habitats. In this framework, the regeneration project of the existing physical space represents an indispensable device to guarantee healthy, comfortable and happy living conditions in beautiful cities where people can live well (Ricci et al. 2020).

It sounds banal but it is not. The transformation of the existing city into the city of the future as an objective of shared quality is a complex operation involving new skills, strategies and projects. the quality of the life. Urbanism from being the science of urban expansion can become the science of regeneration of the existing city. And science, as Carlo Rovelli writes in Seven Brief Lessons on Physics (Rovelli 2016) is above all a visionary activity. Scientific thinking feeds itself on the ability to see things differently than before.

Accepting a condition that only admits the theory of regeneration without replacement or expansion of the building fabric is not a given. In Western countries as in the Far East, incremental and replacement logic continues to represent the main paradigm of city development and transformation. Despite the current social, economic and environmental contingencies, the urban future is still anchored to growth forecasts. But today the scenario is completely different and for developed cities it proposes a stable or negative demographic balance, an ecological transition that admits no exceptions, a time that seems

02 | Permartive masterplan skeme

to stand still and an immense legacy of existing empty spaces to which the urban regeneration project can give sense and new beauty.

The simultaneous action of three decisive factors: the economic crisis, the environmental crisis, and the revolution in sharig information technologies is so profoundly changing our lifestyles and the way we imagine and desire the solid forms of our future that all our design knowledge suddenly becomes inadequate both as an interpretative tool of the current condition and as a device capable of generating new aesthetic qualities and environmental, social, and economic performance. The environmental crisis establishes new levels of shared quality. The economic crisis empties city spaces. The progress of sharing information technologies generates abandonment or, rather, the transfer of functions to an immaterial place that until now needed a physical space to be realised (Bauman 2002).

If all this is about to happen or it s already happening, it is clear that many essential paradigms of the modern, not only that of the close relationship between use and form of the city, or of architecture, are emptied of meaning. The functional rather than performance organisation of the city, the modelling theories, the 'good practices' seem epiphanies of a logic that belongs to another era. Thinking of tomorrow, one could say that what is happening to the most evolved societies as a result of shared information is the possibility of being able to inhabit much more physical space than in the past and not necessarily having to conform it to specific pre-established destinies (Branzi 2010). Quite simply, we have a huge amount of built volume available that is no longer needed or that we do not yet know how to use and that is progressively decaying. The same happens with infrastructure and open spaces. Trento is the first city in Trentino in terms of the size of its building stock and has within it as a volume of empty buildings, the second largest city in Trentino.

Narrative, social action and performance
Leaf Plan, Trento

What is the destiny of urban planning (and more generally of design disciplines) in an era that seems to consider only – or at least with absolute priority – the evolution of intangible spaces and related devices? If today – and in the future increasingly so – the theme of city development is no longer about growth but resilience and environmental quality? When not the construction of the new, but the efficiency and re-signification of existing buildings, become the central issues of building production? This is a major challenge for architectural culture. A challenge that values the existing with conceptual devices that work on the slippage of meaning and new life cycles of living spaces

(Guallart 2012). Aesthetic values remain fundamental, but they are changing rapidly and there is a growing consensus among social and technical actors on three parameters of design for the regeneration of physical space that are not opposed but can be integrated.

Narrative, social action and performance, are criteria that identify an anachronistic design attitude in Agamben's sense, anti-graceful and popular. They emphasise the need to break with a conception of urban development essentially based on the construction of the new. These are viewpoints on the meaning of urban intervention in the age of the present time when the future we dreamed of for cities never comes and is probably no longer what we want, and the existing built space seems to be the last possible context of intervention for better living: the new heritage of cities, a seemingly informal place where nature and traces of previous eras are composed in a landscape dense with meaning and people. The result of this shifting process from the aesthetics of signs to the aesthetics of senses gives beauty to a new form of landscape–city that is probably the only sensible form of inhabiting the physical world today, a space in which nature is the main infrastructure linking people and quality of life (Waldheim 2016).

The project for the new Trento Plan experiments in practice the same paradigms and, as in Nolli's image of Rome or Rem Koolhaas's map of New York, takes the image of open spaces as the shape of the city: a leaf.

In leaves, the ribs are the conducting vessels, the channels that brings life.

03 | The five challenges

Water and mineral substances from the roots reach the leaves through these channels, are processed into sap and brought back to the ground via the same ways. In Trento, the ribs of the city are the lines, the concretions and the social relationships traced by its open spaces. It is the green and blue infrastructures that organise the system of public spaces and social life. The ribs describe a system of existing and magnetic spaces that continually tends to grow stronger. Their position represents the landscape/environmental corridors that descend from the mountain, the trace of the ancient iditches now underground, the tree-lined avenues, the main lines of urban crossings, such as waiting spaces, unsolved and abandoned places. The green rib system catalyses public education, sports and recreational facilities, spaces for universities, places in the historic city and tends to attract spaces for the new landscape and environmental compensations. It identifies the channels of the continuous aggregation of the landscape/environmental qualities of the city and the favorite places of social life.

This is the structural vision of the framework of research actions in scientific support of the 2016-2020 General Revision to the Trento Plan.

In line with the themes outlined by the European Urban Agenda, Environment, Society, Demography, Mobility, Economy (UN 2016), the plan proposes five challenges for the future and development of Trento. The challenges include short-term and long-term objectives, but unlike them they do not have set deadlines. They are fought day by day with strategic actions and small local changes.

Having achieved one quality objective, the challenge pursues another in an almost metabolic process of continuous improvement of the city's social, environmental, economic and cultural performance. The 5 challenges intercept the main problems and potentials of the city: the activation and regeneration of marginal areas, soil consumption, the role of agriculture (for communities, for the microclimate, for productivity and excellence), the management of water use, landscape, environmental and social aspects, biodiversity, urban climate change (microclimate and urban heat island). These are realised in the transformation of the physical space of the city and can be implemented through various action policies that form the basis of the new PRG.

On these premises, the Strategic Document[1] was drawn up, which identifies the five challenges for the city of Trento declined into 18 objectives and 68 strategies, which in turn refer to the goals proposed by the 2016 European Urban Agenda (Ricci and Favargiotti 2019).

---

1. The Strategic Document was elaborated during 25 thematic and operational meetings by a technical round table made up of representatives of the municipal technical offices, the Professional Associations of the Province of Trento (Architects, Engineers, Geologists, Agronomists and Foresters) and the TUT (Transformazioni Urbane a Trento) research group of the Department of Civil, Environmental and Mechanical Engineering (DICAM) of the University of Trento.

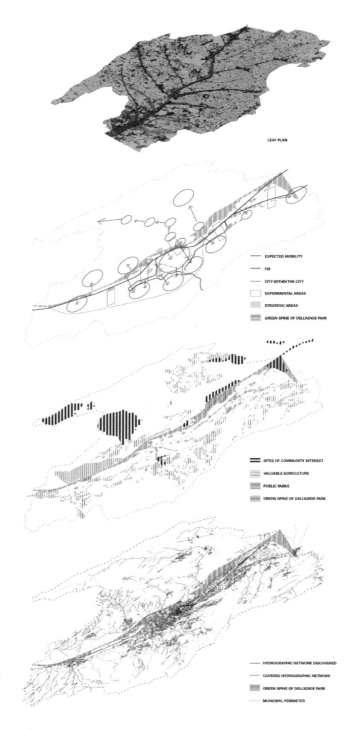

LEAF PLAN

EXPECTED MOBILITY

FBI

CITY WITHIN THE CITY

EXPERIMENTAL AREAS

STRATEGIC AREAS

GREEN SPINE OF DELL'ADIGE PARK

SITES OF COMMUNITY INTEREST

VALUABLE AGRICULTURE

PUBLIC PARKS

GREEN SPINE OF DELL'ADIGE PARK

HYDROGRAPHIC NETWORK DISCOVERED

COVERED HYDROGRAPHIC NETWORK

GREEN SPINE OF DELL'ADIGE PARK

MUNICIPAL PERIMETER

04 | The Leaf layer
of the plan

1. Eco Trento for a sustainable city, based on a network of green areas, on the vitality of agricultural, natural and semi-natural areas that must aim at adaptating to climate change

Trento is an ecological and sustainable city, a green city and a clean city, a city that is attentive to the quality of the landscape, to making the environment attractive, to caring for green spaces by increasing their extension in a systemic perspective, to improving the integrated waste cycle, to reclaiming polluted sites, to incentivising the use of renewable energies, through a balanced consideration of environmental, social and economic components in programming and planning activities. The notion of sustainability applied to the urban scale, in fact, requires the adoption of a planning approach that clearly takes into account the tension that exists between the unsustainable use of resources and the need for their prudent and sustainable management over time. Trento must therefore increasingly characterise itself as a sustainable city, based on a vital ecological system, on a network of green areas extending from the centre to the outer areas, on the vitality of agricultural areas, urban gardens, natural and semi-natural areas. Urban sustainability is also identified in the city's balanced relationship with its surroundings and concerns traffic, water management, waste management, land-use planning, and urban and peri-urban green management. The system of green areas contrasts in a functional and ecological sense with the tangle of infrastructures and anthropic elements that characterises the city's urban mosaic; green areas, also through the formation of corridors, attempt to re-establish ecological balances and functions that are essential for our quality of life. To these prerogatives are added unexpected qualities of city greenery, new functionalities linked to the absorption of dust and heavy metals produced by means of transport and heating systems, the containment of thermal imbalances and meteoric water loss, and new possibilities for economic development linked to the use of renewable energy sources. Trento must therefore aim at energy transition, good use of natural resources, supporting the closure of resource cycles, climate change mitigation and adaptation.

2. Welcoming Trento for the endowment of spaces and places that enable people to meet, to integrate, to improve the quality of life in neighbourhoods and suburbs, as well as to welcome visitors and tourists

A growing city must enhance all its urban areas, with the aim of making peripheral and marginal areas more liveable. Meeting their daily needs means equipping the suburbs not only with excellent connections to the various areas, but also with all essential community services, offering opportunities for aggregation, such as toy libraries, workshops for adolescents, centres for sports or cultural activities that interest the various age groups of citizens.

Trento will therefore be characterised by the endowment of spaces and places that enable people to meet, get to know each other, and integrate those who choose to live permanently or for short periods in the city. As a city that promotes the community's sense of belonging to its living environment, that recognises the different identities present, that encourages social regeneration, supporting the quality of life in neighbourhoods and suburbs. Indeed, redevelopment passes through ordinary but constant interventions that guarantee cleanliness, street maintenance and safety to the neighbourhoods. But that is not all. The active involvement and participation of citizens and associations in the individual neighbourhoods are essential tools for fostering cultural dynamism and the organisation of centres to host and guarantee the development of their activities. The citizens of the suburbs must therefore find a microcosm of services at their disposal and an efficient connective network towards the historic centre and other localities in the area.

3. Accesible Trento to guarantee good supra-local connections by enhancing the places of railway mobility, containing traffic flows and encouraging sustainable mobility

The challenge of sustainable development in urban areas requires reconciling on the one hand the economic development of cities and their accessibility, and on the other hand the quality of life of the inhabitants and the protection of the urban environment, by setting 4 objectives within an integrated approach: smooth traffic flow in cities; smarter urban transport; accessible urban transport; safe urban transport. On a local scale this means promoting slow mobility by enhancing streets, greenways and pedestrian areas as urban places of personal well-being and meeting.

4. Smart Trento to qualify as a competitive and innovative city, which integrates the places of education and research with productive activities

The 'smart city' concept consists above all of a different and new way of using existing resources and presupposes the circulation of ideas, the capacity for social, cultural and functional comparison and assimilation as a collective orientation, desired and shared by the entire community. Trento therefore has the potential to qualify itself as a competitive and innovative city, which integrates places of education and research and productive activities, which adapts spaces and structures to new work models, which provides space for new activities, creativity and young people. The city must found its attractiveness on the urban quality and the quality of the environment to which belongs, on a high life standard supported by personal and business services, on cultural, leisure, sports and university opportunities.

5. Bella Trento to capture the beauty of urban spaces and landscape as a common good and resource on which to base the well-being and attractiveness of the community

A city committed to the preservation (identification, protection and conservation) and enhancement (promoting knowledge and ensuring the best conditions for public use and fruition of its heritage constituted, according to the Cultural Heritage and Landscape Code, actively contributes to 'preserving the memory of the local community and its territory and promoting the development of culture'. The protection and enhancement of natural and cultural resources are of strategic importance to promote local sustainable development, considering it a decisive factor in improving the quality of life of local residents and attracting more visitors from Italy and abroad. The objective is to implement actions that make social and cultural capital a driver of sustainable development by relaunching the distinctive features of Trentino's history, industriousness and knowledge. Because the Plan is a cultural product in its oscillation between the rights and duties of a community, in describing its present and expectations for tomorrow.

Three actions for the plan

The new Master Plan revision offers a response to the new question of design competence at the various scales in the field of ecological urbanism, the themes of landscape, environmental and construction sustainability, mitigation, climate change, resilience, collaborating to define a planner and manager figure capable of combining skills of architecture, territory, environment and contemporary technologies. It proposes an offer tailored to the new needs of society while respecting the local alpine context and the guidelines of European programmes. The preliminary actions of the Plan focus on the management of the ecological and sustainable project, the reading and understanding of complex contemporary landscapes, natural and man-made ecosystems, together with the tools to analyse it in economic terms (Ricci 2020).

In particular, three actions are driving the debate on the future of Trento.

The Plan as narrative expresses the need to give meaning to the project of the existing, making people discover with new eyes what is already there. It reflects a concept of urban planning capable of listening, welcoming, annexing

05 | View of the city center from Italcementi hill. Photo by Matteo Aimini 2020

the tensions of the city and its inhabitants. A narrative that stages meanings, rediscovers sensuality, reactivates the beauty of urban centres.

The Plan as 'performance', the idea of scientific and technological innovation, the principle of urban aesthetics. Performance urbanism opposed to zoning puts at the centre of transformations not the functions but predictable innovative results in ecological terms. Not only that, it makes the territory welcoming for the sustainable development of urban life. The mitigation of major climate changes, the relational quality of public spaces, energy and waste cycle issues, mobility, knowledge as an engine for growth, territory as a smart grid of ecological, landscape and social values. A tool that promotes a new vision of quality of life based on shared and continuously verifiable objectives.

The Plan as 'social action' interprets the spirit of the times that leads us to overcome traditional participatory processes, taking direct part in the conception and design phases of the urban planning tool. Conceiving planning as an open source system realises an objective of social emancipation and increases the contribution of competence. This idea removes the Plan from authorship, by sharing the creative process and its implementation phase. Ideas and actions become common good by involving the technical skills present in the area and the experiences of those who live in the city. In all of this, the PRG must be future-oriented: it is a promise of work, of development, but also of happiness.

This research project aims to support the update of Trento's General Urban Plan, by proposing a systematic approach to territorial governance based on resilient and adaptive urban planning tools. The research group is multidisciplinary and the approach of the study relies on shared knowledge and cooperation between the researchers, the Municipality and the practitioners by sharing experiences to understand the complexity of Trento and by collaborating to enable new insights for decision-makers. The proposed urban plan offers an adaptive and incremental tool to develop the town in a sustainable way. Being based on three main pillars – narrative, performance, shared action – it aims to provide a guideline to coordinate the city's development with future challenges. The city plan draws on the vision of the town, namely "Trento Leaf Plan", which has an important communicative role by clearly setting out the ecological transition on future development, and defines strategies to combine the vision with the urban challenges.

The intervention themes are those of the quality of life, of the ecological and social roles of open and green spaces in the city, of the mitigation and adaptation to climate change, of social inclusion, sustainability of development, abandonment recycle, sustainable infrastructures and built spaces. It tends to the composition of an ecological mosaic, of a projective and visionary collage of landscape and urban quality that can define the new shape of the city to a landscape dimension, which brings together the urban and the rural in a single metabolic icon representative of the new quality of its habitat. This visionary and metabolic planning instrument is a project that works by challenges to be continuously faced to meet the shared quality goals. The activation of the ecological transition processes aims to involve the environmental performance of the city in relation to the quality of social life, the development of the sense of belonging of the resident populations and the attractive capacities of the city of Trento.

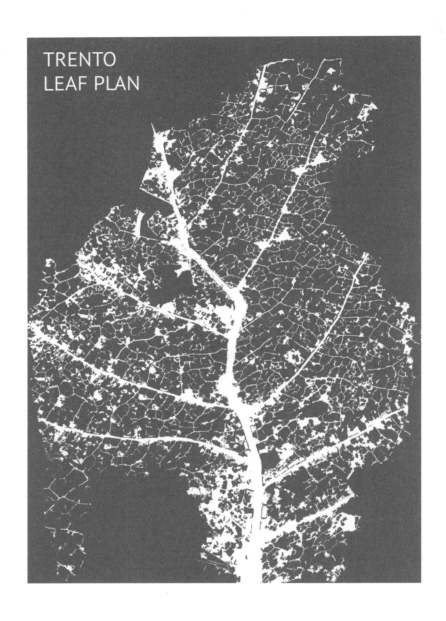

TRENTO
LEAF PLAN

06 | Leaf Plan: visionary mosaic of shared landscape and urban quality, between urban and rural. TUT Research Group - Trento Urban Transformation, DICAM, UniTrento2017.
Graphic processing Silvia Mannocci.

Bibliographic references

Branzi, Andrea. "For a Post-Environmentalism: seven suggestions for a new Athens charter." In *Ecological Urbanism*, edited by Mohsen Mostafavi and Gareth Doherty, Harvard University Graduate School of Design, Lars Müller Publishers, Baden, Switzerland, 2010, pp. 12–13.

Bauman, Zygmunt. *Liquid modernity*. Laterza, Rome, 2002.

European Commission. *New Leipzig Charter-The transformative power of cities for the common good*, 2020. Available at: https://ec.europa.eu/regional_policy/sources/docgener/brochure/new_leipzig_charter/new_leipzig_charter_en.pdf [accessed 19.01.2021].

Guallart, Vicente. "City Protocol - Anatomy of City Habitat", initiative promoted and supported by Barcelona municipality and CISCO for the support and development of BIT-Habitat (Barcelona Institute of Technology for the Habitat), 2012. Available at: https://www.youtube.com/watch?v=zs_sNEfzvVY [accessed 27.07.2019].

Legambiente, *Urban ecosystem. Report on the environmental performance of cities 2020*, 2020. Available at: https://www.legambiente.it/wp-content/uploads/2020/11/Ecosistema-Urbano-2020.pdf [assessed 28.01.2021].

Ricci, Mosè, Mathilde Marengo, João Nunes, Areti Markropoulou, Mara Balestri, Gonzalo Delacámara, Sommariva Emanuele, Paolo Picchi, Silvia Mannocci, Maura Mantelli. *Luxemburg Ecological Transition Plan proposal*, 2020.

Ricci, Mosè. "Adapt_ability: The Leaf Plan concept". In *Activating Public Space: An Approach for Climate Change Mitigation* edited by Alessandra Battisti and Daniele Santucci. München: TU München Press, 2020, pp. 65–75. DOI: 10.14459/1543270md2020

Ricci, Mosè; and Sara Favargiotti. "Trento Leaf Plan. Five challenges for urban metabolism", *ECO WEB TOWN*, v. 1/2019, no. 19, 2019, pp. 1–10.

Rovelli, Carlo. *Seven Brief Lessons on Physics*, Riverhead Books, 2016.

United Nations General Assembly. *New Urban Agenda*, New York: United Nations, 2016. Available at: http://habitat3.org/the-new-urban-agenda/ [accessed 10.05.2020].

Waldheim, Charles. *Landscape as Urbanism*, Princeton University Press, 2016.

#Vision

Landscape as design agent: towards an ecological and biodiversity plan

Sara Favargiotti

On Landscape

In 2000, the European Landscape Convention defined "Landscape" as "an area as perceived by people, whose character is the result of the action and interaction of natural and/or human factors" (ELC 2000). The human and social perception of the anthropic landscape is placed at the center of the interpretation as well as of the actions in the territory. Accordingly, landscape design is a valuable resource for regenerating, restoring and renewing urban, peri-urban and rural areas, often obsolete or abandoned. Land recovery and transformation processes find an opportunity in urban agriculture to improve the quality of life in cities, interpreting the abandoned areas as reserves capable of managing climatic, ecological, and social complexities. Indeed, natural areas offer unique and precious resources for cultivating biodiversity by providing ecosystem services and public space of quality and happier lifestyles.

The biodiversity loss has significant impacts to health and well-being. Numerous studies have investigated the impacts of climate change on biodiversity and on human health based on the concept of biophilia intended as the "the innately emotional affiliation of human beings to other living organisms" (Wilson 1993, p. 31). Natural areas and ecosystems can contribute positively to human health in various ways, such as: by providing ecosystem benefits and services that sustain life and regulate against detrimental health effects from climate, floods, infectious diseases, etc.; as botanical sources for both traditional and modern medicines; and by providing direct benefits to physical, spiritual and mental health through time spent in nature (MacKinnon et al. 2019).

Integrating climate change, biodiversity and human health requires new methodological and operational approaches based on inter-and-trans-disciplinary working. Social integration, climate adaptation, enhancement of environmental and ecosystem services (protecting against erosion, facilitating pollination, supporting tourism and biodiversity) grounds the perspective for a sustainable and circular urban regeneration. Within this perspective, the Leaf Plan research promotes an urban plan and design methodology with the care, promotion, and management of landscape at the center. Indeed, the most urgent urban challenges consist of the valorization of landscapes through the preservation of natural ecosystems, the regeneration of "marginal" areas and the promotion of multifunctional landscapes for community, microclimate, productivity, and excellence.

A change of perspective in the opposed relations between city and country leads therefore to an integrated vision of the peri-urban territory that assumes a vital and active role with new productive functions and attractions. This happens in Trento, "a city of landscapes", where the complexity of the territory requires a holistic approach to the territorial policies and urban design, able to properly represent the different challenges and specificities of the territory (Favargiotti 2020).

In Trento, an ecological approach to landscape design represents an opportunity to take care of the lands, by locally supporting actions of mitigation to climate change, risks protection (mainly from floods and storms), ecological connectivity and biodiversity conservation alongside helping to valorize itineraries at different altitudes and for different targets. Biodiversity and healthy natural ecosystems underpin and sustain human livelihoods and well-being by providing essential services such as food, clean air and water, and protection against floods, coastal storms and other natural disasters (Dudley et al. 2010).

This approach can become an opportunity to reconnect society with its landscape identity and geographical characteristics (urban, rural, regional, territorial), make initiatives economically sustainable and scalable, build a comprehensive and flexible framework to guide cities to implement projects adapted to multifunctional use on different scales.

Ecological infrastructure and urban biodiversity

The tenth meeting of the Conference of the Parties (2010), adopted a revised and updated Strategic Plan for Biodiversity (United Nations 2010), including the Aichi Biodiversity Targets, for the 2011-2020 period. At the base of the document there was the position that the human community should be considered as part integral to ecosystems and the mechanisms that regulate them and not as a "disturbing element" of the natural balance.

The rationale behind the plan is that maintaining the biodiversity of a given ecosystem is vital to the productivity of the ecosystems and their ability to provide the services that humans need, such as food security, health, provision of clean air and water, up to local livelihoods and economic development.

The vision of the plan is "Living in harmony with nature" by seeking by 2050 to enhance, conserve, restore and use the biodiversity, maintaining ecosystem services that are fundamental both for a healthy planet and essential for all people. In this framework, the City Biodiversity Index (CBI), or the Singapore Index, has been proposed as a self-assessment tool for cities to assess and compare different cities in their efforts to conserve Biodiversity against individual baselines. The Index of Singapore includes a first section to profile

01 | Open spaces can be designed and managed to encourage ecological continuity and biodiversity like in Jardins Abbé-Pierre – Grands Moulins, Paris 13e. Source: Mairie de Paris, photo by Yann Le Bourligu.

of the city that provides basic information on current urban characteristics such as location, inhabitants, species; the second section containing twenty-three indicators measuring three areas: biodiversity native, ecosystem services provided by biodiversity, and the biodiversity management in the local area.

The use of this index allows comparison with very different cities, which can dialogue and exchange information for the purpose of implementing the use of techniques that have obtained beneficial results. To calculate the index, the analysis concerning biodiversity was carried out, related ecosystem services and the set of biodiversity management procedures implemented by the cities. From this procedure, an overall picture of the quantity and quality of the natural areas present and the management of biodiversity in the area, highlighting its critical issues and potential.

The "Barcelona Green Infrastructure and Biodiversity Plan" (2020) is a strategic plan that defines the commitment of local government in the management of urban biodiversity and green infrastructure, while also encouraging the citizenry to familiarize with the natural heritage and its benefits. The plan starts from an analysis of green infrastructure, considering not only public but also private areas. The mapping highlights several typological areas that have been described with a qualitative analysis based on the subjective perception of the spaces. In addition, a description of the biodiversity was proposed, with

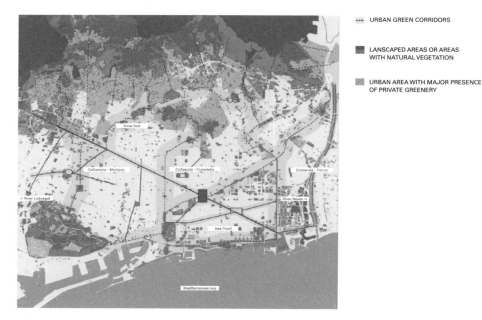

URBAN GREEN CORRIDORS

LANSCAPED AREAS OR AREAS
WITH NATURAL VEGETATION

URBAN AREA WITH MAJOR PRESENCE
OF PRIVATE GREENERY

02 | Barcelona Green Infrastructure and Biodiversity Plan, 2020
Source: Ajuntament de Barcelona

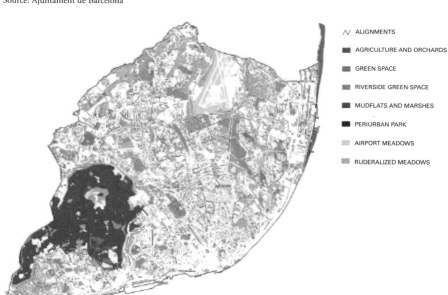

ALIGNMENTS

AGRICULTURE AND ORCHARDS

GREEN SPACE

RIVERSIDE GREEN SPACE

MUDFLATS AND MARSHES

PERIURBAN PARK

AIRPORT MEADOWS

RUDERALIZED MEADOWS

03 | The biodiversity strategic plan of the city of Lisbon, 2020
Source: Câmara Municipal de Lisboa

the species that can be encountered most frequently and the areas that can be recognized as bearers of naturalistic interest.

Information related to the maintenance and management needed for each area have been implements, with the aim of also presenting a management plan for parks and trees along the boulevards, also including a plan for irrigation. From this detailed analysis of the entire ecological infrastructure, the municipality have highlighted the strategic actions in which local government needs to improve the green network, consisting of both ecological corridors and areas possible for intervention.

The biodiversity strategic plan of the city of Lisbon (2020) differs from the others in the analysis model by adopting the Singapore or City Biodiversity Index (CBI). It is structured in two sections: the first proposed a description of the city by including the climate, economy, geology, and population dynamics; the second focuses on biodiversity analysis where the ecological structure (which includes green areas, barriers, natural corridors and wet system), the tree cover and permeable areas have been mapped.

These were associated with a qualitative and quantitative description of the status of urban biodiversity and a breakdown into ecotopes (environmental units) that represent different habitats of species, plants and animals. Based on this analysis, the continuity and fragmentation of the areas has been evaluated by using a surfaces buffer around permeable areas and structural corridors. At the end of the process, a precise overview of the ecological infrastructure and biodiversity situation emerged.

With this knowledge, it has been proposed an action plan with strategies applicable at the local level for monitoring and assessing the evolution of biodiversity as well as for comparison with other cities.

The "Plan Biodiversité de Paris 2018-2024" is particularly interesting for the participatory imprint that involved professionals from various fields and citizens. From this participatory analysis three main actions emerged: inclusion of biodiversity in action plans; knowledge, awareness and support for biodiversity; building, managing and experiencing the city as a resource for biodiversity. For each of these axes, various actions were drawn up possible to be implemented over time and the different figures needed to implement them.

The plan focuses on several areas: from areas dedicated to biodiversity, to the development of urban agriculture, with ecological methods such as agroecology or permaculture. This plan is atypical of its predecessors: the plan does not provide maps or analysis, as the city of Paris had previously activated monitoring of green and blue infrastructure, and it foresees the mapping of black infrastructure, related to light pollution and light and brown infrastructure, concerning ground continuity.

04 | Layers of Trento Leaf Plan natural elements. TUT Research Group - Trento Urban Transformation, DICAM, UniTrento, 2017. Graphic processing Silvia Mannocci and Giulia Zantedeschi.

Landscape agency: a pro-active interdependence among human and nature

From these experiences emerged a trend common to many European cities to include biodiversity and ecosystems within the urban plan and design processes. This procedure emphasize how urban areas also can contribute to the protection of species and ensure ecosystem services, benefit also of increased resilience with a regenerative perspective.

The role of ecological infrastructure and urban biodiversity should include as values and resource of cities and territories, such as: biological diversity, innovation, adaptation to current changes, and well-being. Through the agency of landscape design, people's creativity enables more just and equitable spaces for the community (Ferretti and Favargiotti 2022). Indeed, the landscape design approach is the resource for regenerating, restoring, and renewing urban, peri-urban and rural areas.

Land recovery and transformation processes find an opportunity in open air lands to improve the quality of life in cities, as they are reserves for climate adaptation, ecological transition, and social inclusion. This process becomes an opportunity to reconnect communities with its landscape identity and geographical characteristics (urban, rural, regional, territorial). In order to do so, a pro-active contamination is needed due to the contemporary socio-cultural-economic-ecological conditions and the uncertainties perspectives of multiple possible futures, through the sharing of knowledge and experiences between scholars.

The approach of adaptation is not only proposed to solve the environmental problems, but also to make the city more adaptable to future changes and to connect and improve the ecological value of the landscape (Reed and Lister 2014). Differently from the traditional engineering practice, that mainly relies on controlled systems, the landscape design perspective put the natural material as agent of transformation and as a design element.

The landscape-based strategic approaches described in this contribution are based on the idea of interdependence (Miller and Gibson-Graham 2019) of people and species (plants and animals) can drive local policies for landscape care and heritage regeneration that might lead to a multiplication effect that can increase the positive impact at local scale towards more sustainable and resilient landscapes.

Landscape as common drive territories and cities though a sustainable development in a mutual exchange between research, planning and design to foreseen crucial (critical) changes. A cross-disciplinary approach by integrating architecture, urban design, landscape architecture, engineering in ways that blend the knowledge of construction engineering with knowledge of architectural and urban planning tools, with a balanced learning with practice and theory.

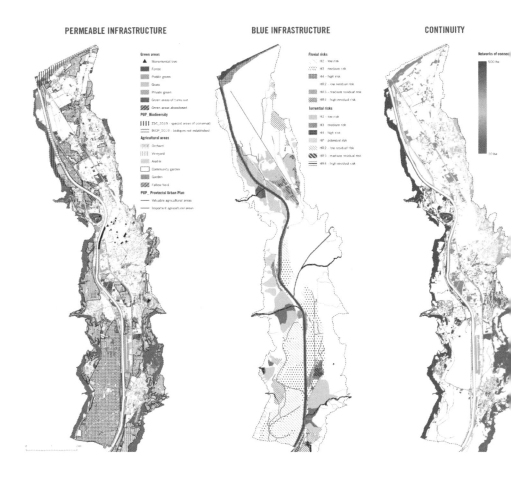

PERMEABLE INFRASTRUCTURE

Green areas
▲ Monumental tree
Forest
Public green
Grass
Private green
Green areas of turns out
Green areas abandoned

PUP_Biodiversity
|||| ZSC_2019 - special areas of conservati
IROP_2019 - biotopes not established

Agricultural areas
Orchard
Vineyard
Arable
Community garden
Garden
Fallow land

PUP_Provincial Urban Plan
Valuable agricultural areas
Important agricultural areas

BLUE INFRASTRUCTURE

Fluvial risks
H2 - low risk
H3 - medium risk
H4 - high risk
HR2 - low residual risk
HR3 - medium residual risk
HR4 - high residual risk

Torrential risks
H2 - low risk
H3 - medium risk
H4 - high risk
HP - potential risk
HR2 - low residual risk
HR3 - medium residual risk
HR4 - high residual risk

CONTINUITY

Networks of connecti
500 ha
10 ha

05 | Urban biodiversity and connectivity; "TRENTO BIODIVER-CITY: towards a plan of biodiversity and ecological infrastructure for the city of Trento", Chiara Frungillo, Master thesis in Architecture and Building Engineering, Trento, 2021, Tutor: Prof. Sara Favargiotti and Prof. Alessandra Marzadri.

DISCONTINUITY

DENSITY

INTEGRATED SYSTEMS

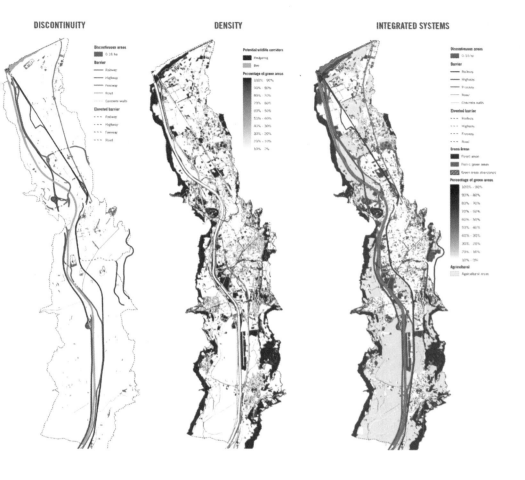

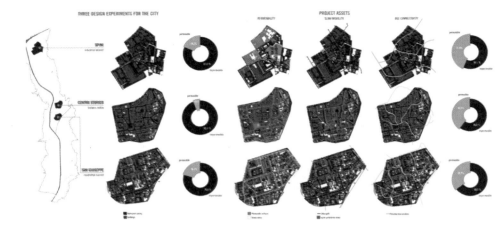

06 | Testing ground for an ecological and biodiverse city; "TRENTO BIODIVER-CITY: towards a plan of biodiversity and ecological infrastructure for the city of Trento", Chiara Frungillo, Master thesis in Architecture and Building Engineering, Trento, 2021, Tutor: Prof. Sara Favargiotti and Prof. Alessandra Marzadri.

07, 08 | Experimental design scenarios: Nature based solutions for redesign the industrial district of Spini in Trento; "TRENTO BIODIVER-CITY: towards a plan of biodiversity and ecological infrastructure for the city of Trento", Chiara Frungillo, Master thesis in Architecture and Building Engineering, Trento, 2021. Tutor: Prof. Sara Favargiotti and Prof. Alessandra Marzadri.

Indeed, to respond to the complexity of the territory, territorial development policies must pursue collective values with territorial qualities by integrating: agricultural production and technological production; territorial and social connectivity; environmental awareness and tourist attraction; natural and cultural diversity; collective spaces, parks and therapeutic green areas; territorial governance, common goods, participation and training. This is how landscape design constitute a multifunctional strategy to develop a more sustainable, interconnected and inclusive habitats.

Designing healthy, resilient, and beautiful cities

The future state of systems, communities, and individuals has conventionally been of interest for decision makers, as well as policy makers, practitioners, and scientists. It might be said that the future has always been unknown. Yet, nowadays, in the age of Anthropocene, this topic is extremely urgent and poses new governance challenges. Risk assessment is more difficult due to the increasing complexity, especially concerning the capability to forecast events or to reliably guide decision making (Miller 2015).

The main threats that affect Western countries, like climate change, environmental degradation, globalization, security, migration, automation, crisis and poverty, are characterized by non-linear, unpredictable, and unstable dynamics.

Lately, the interest in empty spaces, vacant lots, depopulated villages, and obsolete areas in cities and territories and on their recovery is now an inevitable phenomenon in European urban planning, as an emerging dilemma to the well-known debate on the impacts of growing cities and soil consumption in urbanization. Indeed, understanding and qualifying the impact of those transitory urban space patterns in medium and large cities and their metropolitan areas is a fundamental concern as the growing challenges need urgent measures to ensure human well-being and cities livability and to reactivate the rural-urban metabolism (Favargiotti and Pianegonda 2021; Pianegonda et al. 2022).

To do so, the contamination of disciplinary boundaries between landscape, architecture, urbanism, ecology has expanded and redefined the practice of designers and their field of operations. Following this, such relevant themes as uncertainties, climate change, resilience, urban adaptation, nature-based solutions, call for a re-definition of design methodologies in public and private practices. It can do so through sharing knowledge, data, perspectives, and design experiences among the fields of urban, landscape and ecological design, as well as environmental and social studies.

DESIGN TOOLS

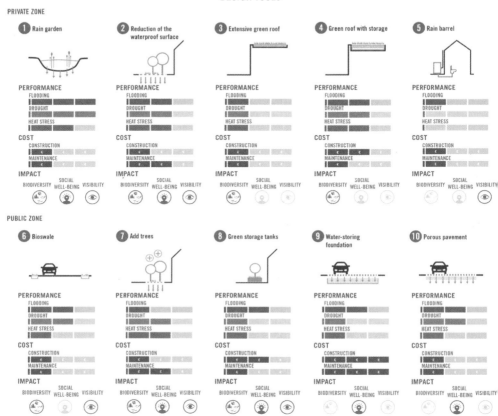

09 | Design tools; "TRENTO BIODIVER-CITY: towards a plan of biodiversity and ecological infrastructure for the city of Trento", Chiara Frungillo, Master thesis in Architecture and Building Engineering, Trento, 2021, Tutor: Prof. Sara Favargiotti and Prof. Alessandra Marzadri.

The Leaf Plan constitutes a methodological approach to shift from traditional planning based on zoning, to more flexible and adaptive planning tools, capable of addressing the societal challenges. It is the baseline to introduce an approach based on challenges that can be developed through multiple actions.

With the Leaf Plan we are promoting a new perspective and design approach in response to urban challenges to rethinking policies and spaces through new paradigms and models guided by strategies of spatial adaptation to change and time.

Underneath a holistic vision of the Leaf Plan, an ecological framework for the city transformation, we offer intertwined landscape and urban design strategies and tools capable to promote the ecological transition as well as to improve the well-being of communities.

Bibliographic references

Council of Europe, *European Landscape Convention*, European Treaty Series n 176, 2000. Retrieved online at https://rm.coe.int/1680080621.

Dudley, Nigel, Sue Stolton, Alexander Belokurov, Linda Krueger, Nik Lopoukhine, Kathy MacKinnon, Trevor Sandwith, and Nik Sekhran. *Natural solutions: protected areas helping people cope with climate change.* Report IUCN/World Bank/WWF, Gland, 2010.

Favargiotti, Sara, and Angelica Pianegonda. "The foodscape as ecological system. Landscape resources for r-urban metabolism, social empowerment and cultural production." In *Urban Services to Ecosystems: Green Infrastructure from the landscape to the Urban scale*, edited by Chiara Catalano, Maria Beatrice Andreucci, Riccardo Guarino, Francesca Bretzel, Manfredi Leone, Salvatore Pasta, Future City / Urban and Landscape Perspectives, Springer, 2021, pp. 279–295.

Favargiotti, Sara. "Re-Cool Trento. Designing blue and green flows for a hot city." In *Activating*

Public Space. An Approach for Climate Change Mitigation, edited by Battisti Alessandra and Daniele Santucci, Technische Universität München, Fakultät für Architektur, München, 2020, pp. 129–140.

Ferretti, Maddalena, and Sara Favargiotti. "Commons in Marginal Landscapes. Collective practices for an alternative narrative and use of common spatial resources in peripheral landscapes." *Ri-Vista* 2022, 19, 2022, pp. 176–189.

MacKinnon, Kathy, Chantal van Ham, Kate Reilly, and Jo Hopkins. "Nature-Based Solutions and Protected Areas to Improve Urban Biodiversity and Health." In *Biodiversity and Health in the Face of Climate Change*, edited by Melissa R. Marselle, Jutta Stadler, Horst Korn, Katherine N. Irvine, Aletta Bonn, Springer, Cham, 2019, pp. 363–380. Retrieved online at https://doi.org/10.1007/978-3-030-02318-8_1 [accessed 19.08.2022].

Miller, Ethan, and Gibson-Graham J. Katherine. "Thinking with interdependence: from economy/environment to ecological

Livelihoods." In *Thinking in the World*, edited by Jill Bennett and Mary Zournazi, Bloomsbury, New York, 2019.

Miller, Riel. "Learning, the Future, and Complexity. An Essay on the Emergence of Futures Literacy." *European Journal of Education* 50 (4), 2015, pp. 513–23.

Pianegonda, Angelica, Sara Favargiotti, and Marco Ciolli. "Rural-Urban Metabolism: A Methodological Approach for Carbon Positive and Circular Territories." In *Sustainability* 2022, 14(21), 2022.

Reed, Chris, and Nina-Marie Lister. *Projective Ecologies*, Actar New York, 2014.

Wilson, Edward O. "Biophilia and the conservation ethic." In *The biophilia hypothesis*, edited by Stephen R. Kellert and Edward O. Wilson. Island Press, Washington, DC: 31, 1993.

#Context

Images of urban change. Potential and prospects of the city of Trento

Bruno Zanon

Renovating our gaze on cities

The city of Trento is immersed in the present, which means that it is living rapid change and is facing the challenges that many other cities and regions are experiencing on a European and global scale. The transformation of the urban form and the displacement of activities are the physical effects of a continual change in the urban economics and in the way people live, move, access services and use space. It is also the effect of a different connection of the local with the upper levels due to the increased mobility of people and goods and to the intangible relationships of our connected society.

Cities need to build their own future, but the phenomena underway require new interpretative tools. Old and new problems cannot be confused, and unexpected opportunities must be appropriately grasped in order to manage the change towards a desirable future.

The case of Trento, a city in northern Italy, among the Alps, was addressed by the research project TUT (Trento Urban Transformations) developed by teachers and researchers of the University of Trento in parallel with the urban planning process conducted by the municipality. The results can be of wider interest, because TUT has focused on a series of issues which are characterizing many cities in the post-industrial society, taking a fresh look at issues considered well-known. In particular, the research highlighted the following challenges: the reallocation of activities, the reshaping of the urban form, the issues of energy and climate change and the role of nature in the urban space. The approaches adopted have primarily taken into consideration the speed of change – which challenges the consolidated urban design experiences and highlights the growing role of temporary uses – and have advanced the concept of an energy neutral city, the role of ecological services, and the perspective of nature-based solutions. A short description of the steps taken by the TUT project to innovate the gaze and the planning methods must clarify the following points.

First, a vision of the future of the city has been expressed – together with the municipality - in the document: "The future of the city of Trento is being built now". It identified some strands on which research had to be developed, thus orienting the efforts of the administration and the stakeholders.

Secondly, the research project combined the analytical phases with the elaboration of proposals. Up-to-date approaches and methods were adopted to address the challenges and to focus on issues and areas worthy of attention and innovative responses.

Third, the elaboration of projects has helped to demonstrate how innovation can take place. But a preliminary question must be addressed to better frame the description of the analytical gaze proposed.

Planning: what is it for?

The meaning and role of urban planning are being debated. Scholars and practitioners are constantly redefining the scope of the planning practice along with its goals and methods. In particular, there is a lot of frustration when referring to a plan as an overall design of the physical components and socio-economic aspects of the urban system, to be considered as a programme by the local administration, and a set of rules by citizens and economic operators.

In the Italian tradition, the "piano regolatore generale" (the general town planning scheme) combines diverse levels, namely the strategic one, the structural one and the one regarding land-use. In recent decades different models have been elaborated by the single Regions, and more experiences have been developed to appropriately pursue the diverse intentions.

Considering that technical expertise and political roles are combined in planning, what is expected from such a process can be summarized as follows:

— a participatory and collective learning process;
— a discussion on problems to share perspectives;
— the elaboration of visions of the future;
— a help to address the uncertainty about the future;
— a creative process of elaboration of proposals to be defined in different terms (physical, narrative, normative, etc.).

The results can be different, therefore: more political or more technical, design-based or assessment-based, a list of suggestions or a set of rules, etc. In any case, the plan must be a temporary step along a circular path that requires continuous reconsideration of problems, solutions, rules.

These considerations concern both the object of planning (the city, in short) and the method to be applied for its design and governance. In fact, during recent decades an intense disciplinary debate has developed at the national and international levels on the new forms of urbanization and the challenges of territorial governance, which involve different scales and areas of intervention and a multiplicity of actors.

It should be emphasized that the current conditions and processes are different from those on which urban planning was developed, as regards the object of action (the urbanized space), the decision-making process (which areas of intervention), the urban form (urban design), and the regulatory mechanisms (land-use planning) (Zanon 2019).

An interesting aspect of some recent planning experiences concerns the application of action-research approaches, particularly when addressing the controversial conditions of derelict urban areas.

Another key aspect modifying the usual planning approach regards the meaning and role of forecasting future change. In particular, it has been observed that, in general, the tasks and commitments of the different approaches have shifted from forecasting sectorial trends to a more comprehensive view of social, economic and environmental factors (Banister and Hickman 2013). A furtherr concept is expressed by the "backcasting" method, concerned "not with what futures are likely to happen, but with how desirable futures can be attained... in order to determine the physical suitability of that future and what policy measures would be required to reach that point" (Robinson 1990).

In this perspective, planning must be an open process, based on the use of information provided by multiple sources, making use also of the methods and technologies that qualify a "smart city". This allows for building innovative paths to achieve the integration of different processes, the coordination of actors, and the active role of citizens (Zanon 2018).

Interpreting the urban change

The variety of current urban forms and the complexity of the urbanization processes underway require disenchanted interpretations. The usual narratives of the phenomena that characterize the contemporary city, the post-industrial economy and the mobile society do not fully describe the multiple niches of the inhabited territory, which hosts a variety of individuals and communities, together with old and new activities. Furthermore, the environmental complexity of an expanded city deserves attention to unexpected natural values and environmental risks, within the broader theme of climate change.

The contemporary city is no longer reflected in the usual image of the well-defined urban space governed by a socially recognized public authority by means of local institutions and locally-based networks. Recalling observations previously made (Zanon 2013), the shape of European cities has changed dramatically, owing to the enlargement of the urban scale, the interaction with extended social and economic processes, as well as to institutional change. At the same time, the open space is assuming increasingly urban features also when dispersed urbanization forms have arisen.

In short, the change that has taken place can be described along three dimensions:

– The physical dimension, because cities are expanding across the territory in a variety of forms, overcoming the distinction between urban and non-urban and the traditional boundaries among local administrations.

– The functional dimension, because services and activities no longer coincide with the city and are progressively separating from urban government. Services, in particular, are based on agencies and companies operating on sectoral bases, often within market mechanisms no longer related to the local.

– The governance dimension, because traditional top-down, authoritative government implies a strict correlation between spatial scales and functions, while the phenomena to be controlled and the services to be provided are no longer under the control of local jurisdictions (Zanon 2013).

Making use of a terminology widely used in the geographical debate, it can be said that de-territorialisation and re-territorialisation processes are occurring, i.e., a progressive breaking of the links between the local community with the consolidated space and activities and the subsequent reorganization of society and places.

Different scales are involved, from the European to the local ones. EU policies and projects are reshaping the continental geography, overcoming national borders and barriers and reducing distances. The forces of globalization, the post-industrial economy and the reallocation of competencies and power from the states to international institutions on the one hand, and to regions, on the other, are accompanied by a new role of the market, also in the usual areas of public domain. What has changed are the strong ties that connected the political-administrative levels with the territories of their competence. The traditional coincidence of local administration-territory-citizens to be provided with services is fading (Zanon 2013). And this also affects the urban space, which needs to be reorganized, in particular as concerns public facilities.

The urban economy is suffering from the closure or displacement of businesses and functions but can benefit from increased accessibility, immaterial connections and knowledge-based industry. The effects are well known and regard the increasing competition among regions and cities and the change in the urban hierarchy.

Scales and factors of change

The processes of urban change are multifaceted, but some key factors can be identified.

A first one concerns social change. This involves a multiplicity of aspects, from the ageing of populations, to the shrinking of families, to the way people access working places, services, and commerce. Furthermore, a large part of the people living in a city are mobile, attracted by temporary work, study and tourism opportunities. Even in Trento, a medium-sized city that has remained far from major immigration flows, the society is increasingly multi-ethnic and economically differentiated, with the consequent risk of spatial segregation.

Social needs cannot be analysed in the way rational planning used to do in search of urban solutions. Families and homes, children and classrooms, the elderly and social assistance do not cover the demand of a society requiring equal opportunities, more mobility and less traffic, interconnected green areas, safety and security, etc.

And this has to do with urban quality. A complex issue concerning different scales – from the building to the block and the neighbourhood –; the time dimension – understood as the changing use of spaces, maintenance and obsolescence of urban components –; the combination of open spaces and built-up areas, green and paved surfaces, residential and working spaces. Not to mention social segregation, which goes hand in hand with spatial fragmentation.

A second factor concerns the economy, which has radically changed in most European and Western world cities, with the closure of heavy industry or its displacement to emerging countries, with the consequent crisis of many cities, the shrinking of the population and the formation of vast brownfields. Many cities have managed to develop the tertiary economy, but a profound change has affected some sectors, such as commerce (with the closure of many small businesses, the development of shopping centres, and the diffusion of e-commerce) and the rise of the knowledge economy.

A third one concerns the reorganization of the infrastructural system and innovation in the mobility of people and goods. Large-scale projects and new forms of transport management make the "gateways" to states and regions move from borders to infrastructure nodes, in most cases coincident with the major metropolitan areas. At the same time, the enlarged scale of mobility and the privatization processes have stimulated the creation of large companies operating in the upper scale and the proliferation of small enterprises operating in niche markets (Zanon, 2015). The result is an increased offer of mobility, on a flexible basis. The usual role of Trento as a commercial city along the Adige valley, connecting the Mediterranean with Central Europe, must be redefined.

On a local scale, the provision of public transportation must develop a new concept of mobility network, based on cooperation between private and public. As regards the urban form, what is changing is the consolidated role of the mobility hubs (railway stations, bus stations, intermodal centres). At the same time, new technologies are available to provide innovative solutions for short-distance travels by means of people movers or elevators, or by exploiting the information flows produced by the "big data" to manage mobility in a smart way. On the contrary, the material effects of e-commerce must be properly managed.

All these factors affect the structure and shape of the city and how people experience the urban space. In this regard, some fundamentals must be kept in mind, starting with the role of the collective urban space, recalling the lesson of Jane Jakobs.

Other issues to be addressed concern the ecology of the built-up space (green and natural areas, water, waste management), the energy challenge (which requires in particular more local production, the improvement of buildings, the prevention of heat waves), security (in relation to the design of urban spaces).

A number of approaches and methods recently developed can be used in this endeavour. The added value of a research project accompanying an urban planning experience is based on the ability to innovate the way the city perceives itself, considering that perception operates a comparison between reality and the feasible goals and implementable solutions.

Pictures for a knowledge-base urban planning process

The research project TUT developed a series of urban analyses focused on the evaluation of the relationships between local society and urban space. They were intended to contribute to the circular process described above in order to sustain a knowledge-based and, at the same time creative, decision-making process.

The analyses were aimed at providing images and sketches that summarize the acquired knowledge, ready to be reformulated when new insights were available. They are not still images or images of a still life, but they are representations of the dynamics of change, requiring continuous updating. What follows is a selection of the pictures of the proposed change.

Trento, an Alpine city at the heart of Europe

Trento has long been the small capital city of an Alpine land, playing a fundamental role in the relations between the Mediterranean area and central Europe. Over time it has changed its primary functions, from the seat of the Prince-Bishop to a "fortress" at the beginning of the 20th century, marking the border between the Austro-Hungarian Empire and Italy, to a commercial city and then an economic centre hosting a plurality of functions.

The connections with the surrounding space are not simply of a functional kind, based on the supply of goods and materials, but a more identity-based one, relying on the variety of characters of the Alpine landscape and way of life.

The change in the urban role and in the economy has not diminished the shared "Alpine identity" of the city. On the contrary, the development

01 | Trento in the Alpine space

of outdoor activities, the increased quality of local agriculture and a series of initiatives that revolve around the mountain environment have strengthened the Alpine image of the city.

The Alps are an icon of environmental quality, which challenges the way the environment of an Alpine city – of a natural, physical, and social kind - is managed and transformed.

The city of Trento is usually placed at the top of the rankings of quality of life, environmental sustainability, and smartness. But these awards must be the starting point along the path of quality and the improvement of the structural aspects as well as of the communication and knowledge-based tools that citizens and businesses can use in their daily lives and operations.

The central position on the European continent must support the international connections, both material and immaterial, giving the city a bridging role between north and south, different cultures and economies. This implies actively intervening in the cooperation networks among the Alpine regions and states (Alpine Convention, Eusalp, Euregio Tyrol, etc.) and assuming a proactive role in the mega infrastructure projects that cross the province along the "Brenner corridor", defining the city as a connection node. It means also taking advantage of the tourism flows and leveraging on the academic and research centres to reinforce the networks of cooperation and a knowledge-based economy.

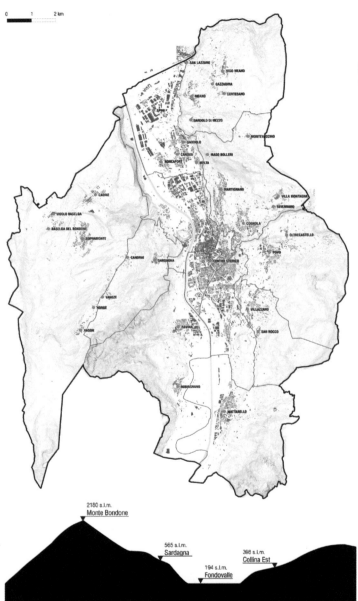

I. Gardolo
Surface   881,79 ha
Population Density   2,43 inh/ha

II. Meano
Surface   1570,25 ha
Population Density   3,18 inh/ha

III. Bondone
Surface   3695,65 ha
Population Density   1,45 inh/ha

IV. Sardagna
Surface   865,52 ha
Population Density   1,27 inh/ha

V. Ravina - Romagnano
Surface   1668,62
Population Density   3,01 inh/ha

VI. Argentario
Surface   1318,84 ha
Population Density   9,49 inh/ha

VII. Povo
Surface   1545,56 ha
Population Density   3,74 inh/ha

VIII. Mattarello
Surface   1640,96 ha
Population Density   3.80 inh/ha

IX. Villazzano
Surface   735,69 ha
Population Density   6,91 inh/ha

X. Oltrefersina
Surface   696,07 ha
Population Density   27,8 inh/ha

XI. San Giuseppe - Santa Chiara
Surface   307,41 ha
Population Density   55,92 inh/ha

XII. Centro Storico
Surface   858,63 ha
Population Density   23,82 inh/ha

60 %
Population residing
in the valley floor

40 %
Population residing
in hilly areas

02 | A polycentric city

A polycentric city

The urban form of Trento combines a central part, around the historical centre which was protected by city walls until the mid-19th century, when the railroad broke the silence and accelerated the change, and a number of neighbourhoods, once country villages and now residential districts.

The recent urban development has meant covering the bottom of the Adige valley with a variety of buildings intended for a mix of functions, and has extended the residence to the hillside. The result is a differentiated urban environment, with some polarities coinciding with the city centre and the main "piazzas" of the former villages, as well as with some shopping malls and new university campuses. High-quality areas and derelict ones, buildings and agricultural land are mixed up. Apart from a number of problems that emerge, in particular as regards the social differentiation of the city, this condition must be considered for the potential it offers, due to the different opportunities to live, work and access services that it provides.

As for the role of the public, great attention must be devoted to the change in the provision of collective services, to the innovation of the commercial sector, to the reallocation of activities, which can dramatically change the way a district operates, even without major physical transformation. The governance of the urban space not only requires intervening on building permits, but also guiding, stimulating and assessing the effects of the stable and temporary uses. Specific attention must be paid to the intermediate spaces between neighbourhoods and the built-up parts, which are often natural areas or valuable agricultural land, served by walking paths.

An evolving urban community

The urban population has shown a constant increase in recent decades, with an intense interchange with the province, other Italian regions and, increasingly, the world. Trento hosts one-fourth of the provincial population, being a hub of services, jobs and other urban opportunities. Intense commuting flows connect the city with the surrounding territory.

As concerns demography, the population is ageing and families are getting smaller, with nearly 40% of them being single-person. This dramatically changes the way people live, how homes must be designed and what services must be provided. The decline of the industrial sector has been counterbalanced by the growing role of the service sector and, in particular, of the university, the research centres, the cultural activities. And tourism has become a key function.

As a consequence, new people arrive, who expect to become citizens, whether they are permanent or temporary inhabitants of the city. In particular, university students need not only an accommodation but a home to fully experience urban life.

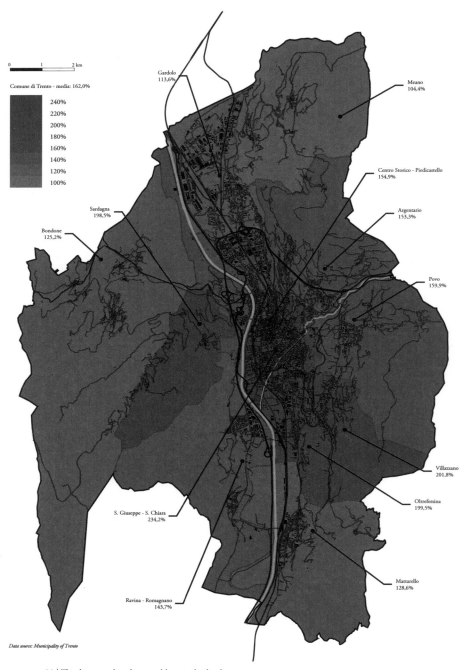

0   1   2 km

Comune di Trento - media: 162,0%

240%
220%
200%
180%
160%
140%
120%
100%

Gardolo
113,6%

Meano
104,4%

Centro Storico - Piedicastello
154,9%

Sardagna
198,5%

Argentario
153,3%

Bondone
125,2%

Povo
159,9%

Villazzano
201,8%

Oltrefersina
199,5%

S. Giuseppe - S. Chiara
234,2%

Mattarello
128,6%

Ravina - Romagnano
143,7%

Data source: Municipality of Trento

03 | The demographic change: old-age index by district

0   1   2 km

Comune di Trento - totale stranieri: 13.288

28%
24%
20%
16%
12%
8%
4%
0%

Gardolo
21,1%

Meano
1,4%

Centro Storico - Piedicastello
27,7%

Sardagna
0,5%

Argentario
4,4%

Bondone
2,3%

Povo
2,1%

Villazzano
1,2%

Oltrefersina
15,5%

S. Giuseppe - S. Chiara
17,7%

Mattarello
3,6%

Ravina - Romagnano
2,4%

Data source: Municipality of Trento

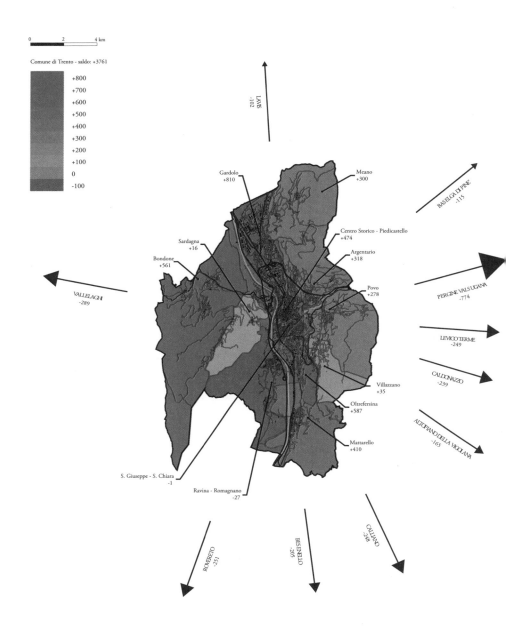

0   2   4 km

Comune di Trento - saldo: +3761

+800
+700
+600
+500
+400
+300
+200
+100
0
-100

LAVIS
-102

Gardolo
+810

Meano
+300

BASELGA DI PINE'
-115

Centro Storico - Piedicastello
+474

Sardagna
+16

Argentario
+318

Bondone
+561

VALLELAGHI
-289

Povo
+278

PERGINE VALSUGANA
-774

LEVICO TERME
-249

CALDONAZZO
-239

Villazzano
+35

Oltrefersina
+587

ALTOPIANO DELLA VIGOLANA
-165

Mattarello
+410

S. Giuseppe - S. Chiara
-1

Ravina - Romagnano
-27

ROVERETO
-251

BESENELLO
-205

CALLIANO
-248

Data source: Municipality of Trento

05 | Demographic changes in the districts and transfers to neighbouring municipalities

52

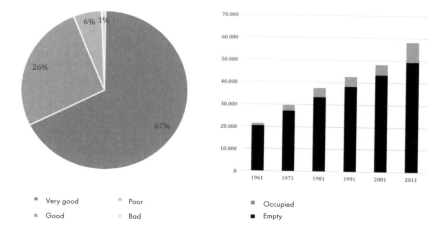

- Very good
- Good
- Poor
- Bad
- Occupied
- Empty

06 | Number of dwellings, occupied and empty; different decades
07 | Residential buildings by state of conservation

The new demographic profile, the new functions and the multiplication of events and temporary uses are producing a change in the way of living and experiencing the city. Therefore, the urban space must be reorganized, considering the emerging social needs.

Homes, buildings, and connective urban space

A city is made up of a multiplicity of components. Not only homes, but also a variety of buildings that host different functions. In the case of Trento, the residential areas cover about 40% of the urban surface, the rest is made up of offices, commercial and industrial buildings, and public facilities. In between is the connective space, which is not simply functional, because it plays a key role in the definition of urban quality. Adding open spaces, infrastructure, public facilities and social housing, the public has to take care of half of the surface of the urban area.

The life cycle of a city expresses different needs in the subsequent periods, and the vitality of the built-up environment follows such a process, leaving apart unused buildings, areas, blocks. These cannot be simply considered as fragments of a city's waste, because they can represent values and memories worthy of consideration and opportunities to provide innovative responses to emerging needs.

Despite the problems of an environmental, social, and urban nature present, these areas can be revitalized by temporary uses or they can be incubators of innovation by activating strategic "urban projects".

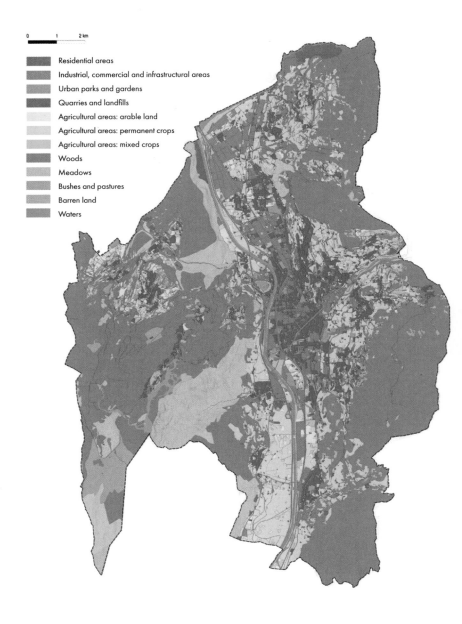

0   1   2 km

- Residential areas
- Industrial, commercial and infrastructural areas
- Urban parks and gardens
- Quarries and landfills
- Agricultural areas: arable land
- Agricultural areas: permanent crops
- Agricultural areas: mixed crops
- Woods
- Meadows
- Bushes and pastures
- Barren land
- Waters

08 | Land-use map

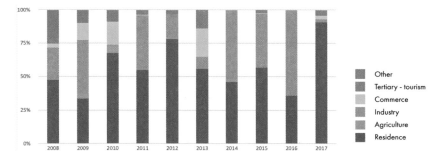

09 | Renovated building surface by use

A recently-built urban district in a former industrial area, whose apartments are not sold because they are not appreciated by the market, is a demonstration that a disenchanted look at urban life is needed. The formal quality, the name of the architect and the qualification of the developer are not enough to adequately satisfy the demand of families and investors.

As concerns the construction sector, it operates following economic cycles, but it is highly sensitive to land-use rules, public investments and incentives. Most of the operations are small-scale, part of an urban metabolism which needs to be sustained and oriented. A lot of public money is being allocated to improve the energy performances of buildings, and this is accelerating widespread improvement. But this piecemeal change does not guarantee a coherent urban space, and a lot must be done to improve the collective space.

An urban space composed also of "weak" elements

The urban space can be redesigned by introducing new elements and giving a prominent role to components usually considered of secondary order. A first case regards green areas. Trento, as an Alpine city, extends its borders onto the surrounding hills and mountains. Urban gardens and parks, agricultural land, natural areas, woods and pastures are different aspects of what must be considered a continuum of manmade and natural spaces. The analysis of the ecological services provided helps to correctly assess the values of these spaces and to avoid considering them as areas of future urban development.

Another factor of change concerns the new forms of mobility. In particular, cycling lanes are supporting soft mobility even in the hilly areas of the city, given the diffusion of e-bikes. Such components must become a structural part of the urban fabric, innovating the Italian tradition of urban design as well as the usual way of managing mobility.

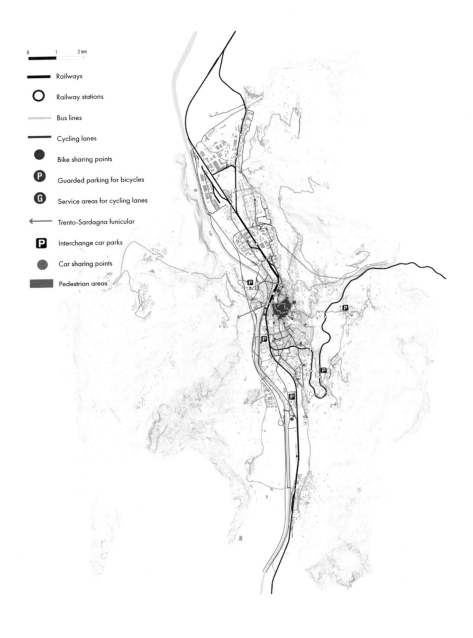

Railways

◯ Railway stations

Bus lines

Cycling lanes

● Bike sharing points

Ⓟ Guarded parking for bicycles

Ⓖ Service areas for cycling lanes

← Trento-Sardagna funicular

🅿 Interchange car parks

● Car sharing points

▬ Pedestrian areas

10 | The infrastructure for a sustainable mobility

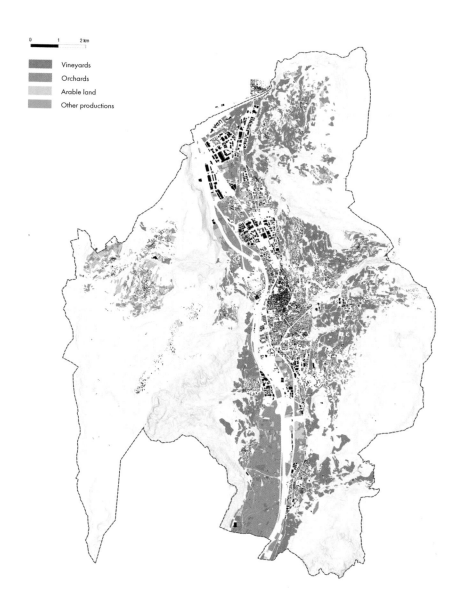

0   1   2 km

- Vineyards
- Orchards
- Arable land
- Other productions

11 | Agricultural areas by type of cultivation

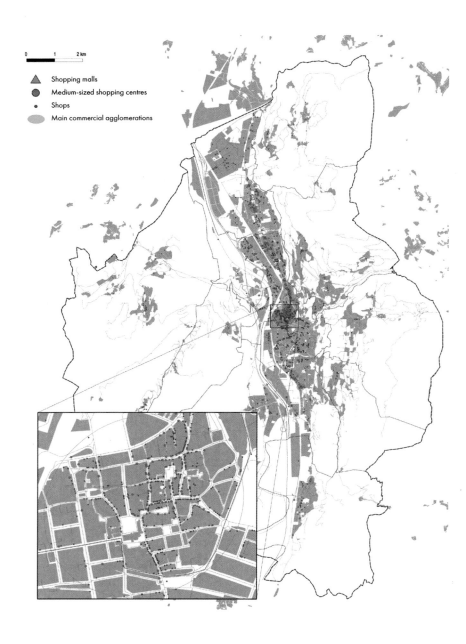

Shopping malls
Medium-sized shopping centres
Shops
Main commercial agglomerations

12 | Commercial distribution

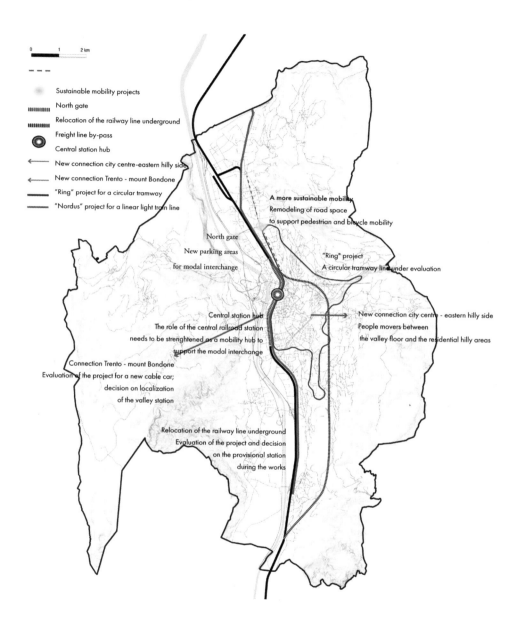

Legend:

Sustainable mobility projects
North gate
Relocation of the railway line underground
Freight line by-pass
Central station hub
New connection city centre-eastern hilly side
New connection Trento - mount Bondone
"Ring" project for a circular tramway
"Nordus" project for a linear light train line

0   1   2 km

A more sustainable mobility
Remodeling of road space
to support pedestrian and bicycle mobility

"Ring" project
A circular tramway line under evaluation

North gate
New parking areas
for modal interchange

Central station hub
The role of the central railroad station
needs to be strenghtened as a mobility hub to
support the modal interchange

New connection city centre - eastern hilly side
People movers between
the valley floor and the residential hilly areas

Connection Trento - mount Bondone
Evaluation of the project for a new cable car;
decision on localization
of the valley station

Relocation of the railway line underground
Evaluation of the project and decision
on the provisional station
during the works

13 | Mobility projects under discussion

In this regard, some proposals to connect the city centre with mount Bondone – a traditional destination for skiing and outdoor activities – with a funicular, as well as with the eastern hillside by means of mechanical systems, can change the relationship centre-suburbs and the open space.

Other "weak components" emerge from the temporary use of spaces, highlighting the potential of areas and buildings considered of little interest.

Growing attention is being paid to the agricultural land surrounding the city and separating the city centre from the suburbs. It is increasingly qualified, producing in particular fruit and grapes for renowned wines. It is also a leisure space frequented daily by people walking and cycling among the greenery.

Urban agriculture, in its different forms, provides important ecological services, from fertile soil preservation, to the production of healthy vegetables and occasions for leisure. And citizens are increasingly involved in amateur production. A challenge regards the defence of agricultural land against urban development.

Hybrid spaces

The contemporary urbanized space is made up of large fringe areas, empty spaces, transition zones: These areas are no longer and not yet urban, but they do not always need to be built. They are hybrid spaces, in many cases presided over by responsible communities, and are endowed with peculiar values – in particular of an ecological nature – which need to be understood and protected. In these contexts, there are usually conflicts between the diverse possible uses of space and resources. The inadequate urbanization processes that have taken place over time, characterized by a varied use of space, require an in-depth analysis of the ongoing phenomena and the elaboration of new technical skills to develop new urban design perspectives and a more effective regulation of land use (Zanon 2019).

An attractive city, where new things happen

In recent times, Trento has succeeded in becoming a tourist destination and in innovating the urban scene by organizing events, festivals and meetings. As an Alpine city, Trento is located in a province where tourism has long been developed, but it has lacked ways to attract visitors. In recent times, the organization of numerous events – of a tourist, cultural and sporting nature – has produced a new image of the city, starting to attract visitors. The consequences concern both the physical structure of the city and the way in which the spaces are used and the activities managed.

A city of knowledge

The city, after the decline of heavy industry, has strongly developed the service sector, in its various forms. In particular, higher education and research have acquired a primary role, since the success of the university and some research centres has turned Trento into a "city of knowledge". These institutions not only provide just a service for the education of the local younger generations, as they have gained national and international recognition, thus attracting students, researchers and teachers from outside. The effect on the local economy is important, qualifying the industrial production, the public administration and innovating how services are provided.

Urban quality is pivotal for a "city of knowledge", because the ability to attract scientists and students depends on offering a range of material and intangible conditions, from large-scale accessibility to local mobility, from quality primary and secondary schools to housing, public services and social life. And the presence of museums, theatres, festivals, etc., some of which connected with the university, provides an occasion for a number of cultural events.

What smart city?

Trento has long been working on the perspective of becoming a "smart city". A number of concrete actions, during the last few years, have been carried out, beyond the usual political rhetoric. It is a project well connected to the European framework and to specific EU-funded projects, as well as to an initiative of the network of Italian municipalities.

A smart city (and territory) is expected to make intensive use of knowledge and up-to-date technologies to manage complex issues in order to provide quality services for its citizens and create an innovative environment supporting sustainable development. A variety of actors must be coordinated, and "governance" is the keyword to appropriately coordinate actors and actions.

The commitment of the city of Trento concerns the improvement of the services furnished to citizens and enterprises and the quality of life. It implies a participatory process involving citizens, institutions and stakeholders.

A number of results have been achieved, in particular as regards the administrative mindset - more outcome-oriented - and some innovative services, centred on the access to municipal data and to the activation of smart tools. In particular, a number of apps can be downloaded from the municipal website to interact with the municipal administration by accessing information and services. In particular, it is possible to consult public transportation schedules, buy tickets, pay parking fees, and use the bike sharing service (Zanon 2018).

Towards a sustainable, inclusive, accessible, smart and beautiful city

The city of Trento is facing tough challenges. The problems recently raised by the pandemic and by the complex international situation increase the level of difficulty posed by the rapid change in the socio-economic profile of the city and in the methods of managing an urban space in transition.

The vision expressed in the preliminary document envisaged a sustainable, inclusive, accessible, smart and beautiful city. This perspective can be achieved by developing a knowledge-based economy and supporting a collaborative local society, capable of bringing together different actors operating in various fields of intervention towards a common project. Planning is a key tool, in this regard, since it is expected to help to understand the change taking place, define a shared perspective and a set of innovative solutions, coordinating all the stakeholders.

The analytical phase conducted as part of the TUT research project proposed a number of images of the phenomena occurring, providing a synthesis that can help to progress in the complex steps of designing a path towards a sustainable urban environment based on better integration between man-made and natural spaces, built-up and green areas, as well as on a better use of energy. What is expected is an inclusive and stimulating urban space for people who choose Trento as their city.

Bibliographic references

Banister, David and Hickman Robin. *Transport futures: thinking the unthinkable,* Transport Policy, vol. 29, 2013, pp. 283–293.

Robinson, John B. *Futures under glass: a recipe for people who hate to predict.* Futures, vol, 22(8), 1990, pp. 820–842.

Zanon, Bruno. *Scaling down and scaling up processes of territorial governance. Cities and regions facing institutional reform and planning challenges,* Urban Research & Practice, vol. 6(1), 2013, pp. 19–39.

Zanon, Bruno. *Territorial Cooperation and Multilevel Governance in the Brenner Base Tunnel Project,* in: S. Fabbro (ed.), Mega Transport Infrastructure Planning. European Corridors in Local-Regional Perspective, Springer, Cham, Heidelberg, New York, Dordrecht, London, 2015, pp. 99–122.

Zanon, Bruno. *Riabitare i luoghi,* in: Camilla Perrone, Michelangelo Russo (a cura di) *Per una città sostenibile. Quattordici voci per un manifesto,* Donzelli, Roma, 2019, pp. 105–120.

Zanon, Bruno. *Territorial Governance and Mobility Management. A Smart Perspective for an Alpine City,* in: Papa, R., Fistola, R., Gargiulo, C., (eds.), Smart Planning: Sustainability and Mobility in the Age of Change, Springer, Cham (CH), 2018, pp. 215–230.

#Context

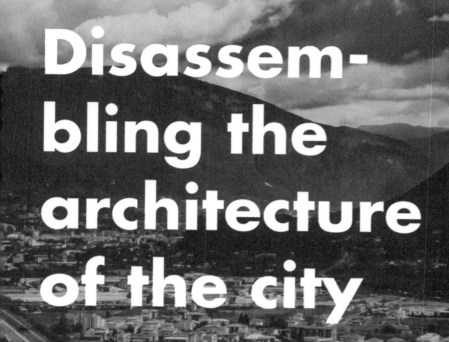

Disassem-bling the architecture of the city

Matteo Aimini

Disassembling Trento

The operation of disassembling the territory of Trento can be of help in introducing the physical dimension of the city, addressing the issue of the relations between urbanisation and the landscape through the lens of photography, drawings and the reading tools associated with the disciplines of design.

This series of operations mainly describes the fabrics of the "città normale", a different concept compared to the Ordinary city (Amin and Graham 1997) or the Generic city (Koolhaas 1995) involving those portions of urbanity that are not affected by certain exceptionalities and not for this reason scarcely deserving of attention.

The "Città normale" is located outside the historic centre (an exceptional moment) and draws with its own character, geometry, rules and the development of about two-thirds of the municipal surface. In this area from north to south, from east to west, are hidden the many challenges that Trento will have to face in the future.

De-layering, classifying and defining the state of the art is a methodological process articulated in stages, and it starts with the definition of the first phase called "Layer reading", a tool that proposes a possible interpretative key for understanding Trento's urban landscape.

The classification of the elements was based on the surveys known as the "Trento Grand Tour", which consisted of a first air photographic campaign covering the entire territory. This practice is directed towards the creation of word clouds and some study parameters such as: the physical elements that make up the landscape; the relations between them and the places on which they insist. Starting with the panoramic photos taken with drones, the dominant "Five Characters" traces possible 'natures' in which to work and to implement the challenges arising from the plan, while the "The Grains and Fabrics" examines the physical elements of the built-up and of the open space.

Subsequently, the photographic narrative at the human level of the "Città Normale" was carried out at a later stage, combining the plan's areas of interest, emergencies, latencies and the 'normality' of the landscape as perceived by people's eyes, generating four possible parameters and reading categories such as Natures, Routes, Artefacts and Perspectives.

The conclusions are summed up in the "Reasoned areas" that recaps and frames some of the priority issues that emerged from the study, like the needs for open space planning, the strategic infrastructure node, the transformation of the Brennero-Adige market road, and finally the Great Areas to the south in a state of temporary disuse.

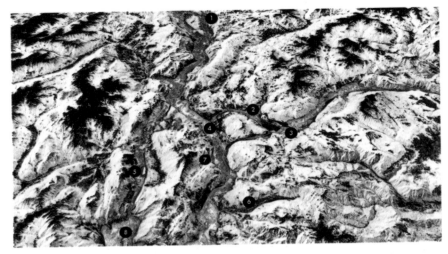

01 | **Adige Valley.** 1 Bolzano | 2 Pergine | 3 Levico | 4 Trento 5 Vezzano | 6 Folgaria | 7 Rovereto | 8 Riva del Garda

02 | City shape of Trento

Context and critical issues

Trento could be defined as a "Metropoli gentile" (Bonomi and Masiero 2014) for its pleasant and natural environment in which to live and produce, for its high standards of living and for its per capita income, which is among the highest in Italy [1]. In particular, Trentino's capital city is located in the Adige valley, in a median position in relation to Verona (in the south) and Bolzano (in the north), at the crossroads of the heads of the Valsugana valley, which runs in a southeasterly direction and connects to the Veneto region, and the valley system that descends towards Lake Garda and the Giudicare valleys, which join the province of Brescia, located in the southwest (Figure 1).

Considering its capillary system of infrastructural connections from north to south, from west to east, fast or slow as they may be, the network surrounding Trento proves to be extensive and ramified, capable of generating a full-fledged system of control that develops and connects polarities innervating all the other more peripheral valleys, centralising strong flows on itself. This dimension expands the city's strength beyond its municipal administrative boundaries, generating a sort of metropolitan area extended between the valley, the plain and the mountain dimension.

In the framework of a possible "MetroMontano" context (Barbera and De Rossi 2021), the Trentino valley city records a largely consolidated geographical and spatial condition that today sees the valley, hill and mountain urban structures working as a single body, sometimes solid and compact, casually porous due to abandonment and highly fragmentary at the margins. Since the post-war period, all of the city's fabrics have rapidly undergone important transformations, such as the transition from the typical socio-economic structure of a mountainous territory to a post-industrial economy, passing through the development of a significant secondary sector.

The urban shape of Trento (Figure 2) changed radically in the transition from the core of the walled city on the banks of the Adige in the mid-19th century to an expanded city at the turn of the 20th century. The rapid post-war expansion generated a variety of patterns and interventions not all clearly planned and governed, producing a sprawling, capillary and problematic kind of urbanisation that defines much of today's urban fabric.

At the turn of the 2000s, the definition "archipelago city" (Mioni, Bocchi, and Zanon 2000) was coined to underline the territorial and morphological articulation, marked by the presence of the ancient autonomous hillside municipalities but also by the coexistence of a plurality of small multiplicities evolving rapidly and contributing to the integration between the centre, the valley and the suburbs that grew up around the old villages.

The processes of the modern transformations and the progressive extension of the infrastructure system over the past decades have completely changed the connections between the city centre and the surrounding area.

The change in the provincial economy, industrialisation, services, the construction of the Brennero motorway and the expansion of the provincial road system have supported a phase of expansion that has pushed the small towns to the limit, merging once isolated centres and engulfing the entire city of Trento in a shapeless and inhomogeneous suburbia. It is predominantly a polycentric urban system, pivoting between the cities of Trento and Rovereto and encompassing numerous other localities, especially to the north, where large and waterproof industrial clusters were considerably strengthened in the second half of the 20th century.

The 'extending city' envisaged by the planning documents of the Provincia Autonoma (Giovanazzi and Franceschini 2012) in the 1960s and 1970s has only partially become spaces of urban quality and opportunity, assuming instead, in the Adige valley bottom, the connotations of the usual disordered

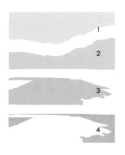

Reading diagram
Decomposition of photographic layers

1 Atmospheric element
2 Rocky backdrop
3 Compact settlement
4 Permeable soil

01 | Industrial plate

Reading planes:
Agricultural plots
Permeable green interlocked
Industrial production fabric
Interporto and pulverised settlements,
Rocky outcrop of Mount Terlago

Location and coordinates of observation point
Spini di Gardolo - 46°07'31.2 "N
11°06'38.7 "E

02 | Geometries of the edges

Reading planes:
Agricultural plots
Residential fabric and hilly settlement filaments
The heights of Camparta Alta

Location and observation point coordinates
Mouth of the Avisio stream - 46°07'30.9
"N 11°06'39.0 "E

03 | De-layering the perceived landscape

mass of the urban periphery which draws a conurbation that gathers almost half of the provincial population (Mioni, Bocchi and Zanon 2000).

Rapidly over the last decade, there has been a shift from the 'archipelago city' to an 'archipelago of shrapnel' of urban, suburban and agricultural types. This widespread condition of fragments in the city also concerns the great processes of territorial transformation that took place in the past and were poorly absorbed by a perpetually stalled present. The new condition that the landscape and the city of Trento are experiencing registers a series of not insignificant critical issues for the near future of the entire territory.

The emerging of critical topics, some structural, others systemic, outlines a series of challenges and problems that the municipality will have to face in the coming decades, endowing itself with unconventional tools to deal with them. The following paragraphs provide reading tools and possible interpre-

03 | Infiltration and Insertion

Reading planes:
Agricultural plots of valley, hillside and slope woodland vegetation
Residential, industrial, hillside dust and road infrastructures
The heights of Camparta Alta and Bassa and Mount Paganella in the background

Location and observation point coordinates
Doss di Lamar - 46°07'31.2 "N
11°06'38.7 "E

04 | Fragments and Saturation

Reading plans:
Agricultural plots and green fragments
Industrial and residential production fabric
Valley relief system

Location and observation point coordinates
Spini di Gardolo - 46°07'38.4 "N
11°06'04.9 "E

tative keys for the emergencies of the metropolitan landscape and the territory in general.

Layer reading

Layer reading develops an initial critical and synthetic analysis of the characteristics of the Trento landscape, investigating, through photographic re-elaboration, the spatial dimension, physicality and relationships of the elements present in the urban and landscape structure of the city of Trento (Figures 3, 4). Anticipating and providing an interpretative key to the "Trento Grand Tour" photographic campaign. The tool of the digital collage (Corner 2013) attempts to break down and simplify the images, and it is unquestionably useful in understanding and restoring the weights, measures, and relationships in the field. If we bind such a tool to categories for reading and subdividing the ima-

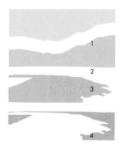

Reading diagram
Decomposition of photographic layers

1 Atmospheric element
2 Rocky backdrop
3 Compact settlement
4 Permeable soil

05 | Commercial plate

Reading plans:
Permeable green interlocking fabrics
Plates of commercial services and urban residential fabric and road infrastructure
On the left the Marzola, Finocchio and Zugna peaks and on the right the Bondone.

Location and observation point coordinates
Melta Park - 46°05'54.3 "N 11°07'01.7 "E

06 | Adige-City Relationship

Reading plans:
Agricultural plots, riparian vegetation and slope woodland vegetation
Diffuse low and medium-density urban fabric and road infrastructure
Marzola and Finocchio peaks in the background.

Location and observation point coordinates
Roncafort south - 46°05'25.0 "N 11°05'50.7 "E

04 | De-layering the perceived landscape

ge, we obtain, as in this case, the identification of four descriptive parameters:

a) The Atmospheric element that determines and modifies the entire perceived landscape, through light and different conditions;

b) The rocky backdrops, unavoidable elements of the city, silent and in the background, with the peculiar shapes of the sinuous hills or in the presence of bristly rock masses that trace and encircle the horizon with their presence;

c) The consolidated building draws that solid mass, sometimes compact or porous, of a regular or fringed shape that represents the geometries of the built-up area, contributing to the emergence of the essential form of the built-up area;

d) The permeable soil, the great natural carpet on which everything lies, the valley floor with its dense woodland vegetation, orderly agricultural plots and fragments trapped by the consolidated urban fabric. Observing the set of collages shown in sequence is like taking a journey that crosses the city and its surroundings from north to south, touching its edges and borders.

07 | The apparent continuity between the hill and the valley

Reading plans:
Agricultural plots and wooded hillside vegetation
Low-density urban fabric, university facilities and consolidated city in the background
Rocky backdrop of Monte Bondone.

Location and coordinates of observation point
Povo - 46°03'58.4 "N 11°09'20.0 "E

08 | Pulviscular aggregates

Reading plans:
Agricultural plots, riparian strips and slope vegetation
Low-density urban fabric, road infrastructure and airport
On the left Palon and Paganella peaks and on the right Camparta Alta and Bassa.

Location and observation point coordinates
Forte Alto, Mattarello - 45°59'52.4 "N 11°08'07.5 "E

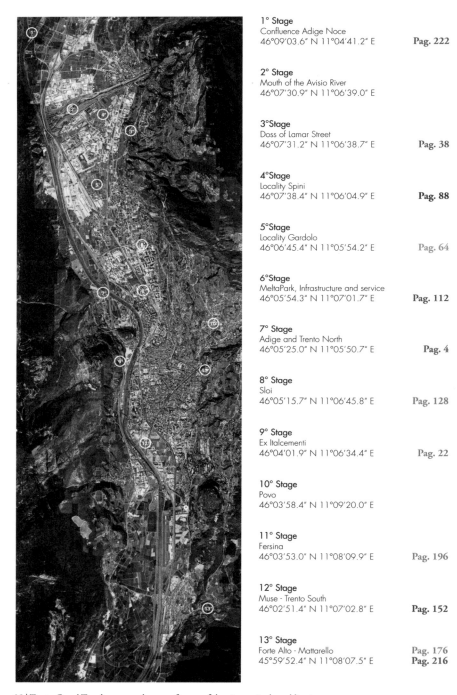

05 | Trento Grand Tour keymap and pages reference of the pictures in the publication.
Aerial footage by Mirco Cecchi and Matteo Aimini

Trento Grand Tour

From far-off times, starting with the 19th-century SAT photographic campaigns, through the experiments in documentary photography of the 1960s and 1970s, up to the photographic journey commissioned by the Province to Gabriele Basilico at the dawn of the 21st century and the more recent experiences promoted by the Autonomous Province of Trento's Department for Territorial Cohesion, the TSM (Trentino School of Management) and Step (School for Territorial and Landscape Governance) in collaboration with Italia Nostra (Curzel and Toffolon 2015), it can be understood how the issues of the landscape, its identity and mode of representation play an important role and how strongly it is felt by the communities that live and perceive this territory every day.

Photography therefore, appears to be a current and important tool for understanding and critically reading the landscape in the areas of study that concern the region, and it must not be excluded from the considerations concerning the revision of the plan. From here the need to stop the present, or at least a part of it, recording de facto the development phase in which the city and the articulation of the nearby territories are in.

The meaning of this work consists of the attempt to foresee a future that would not be abstract, but based on the real conditions of the existing situation. For this reason, a targeted recognition of the municipal area was carried out (Figure 5). Some may argue the futility of such work, as the digital and the satellite cartography provide similar if not more accurate information. Instead, the photographic dimension has the power to restore a unique and unrepeatable three-dimensionality, bringing out more strongly the aesthetic value of the landscape and its issues, contributing to the possibility of formulating innovative reports to support planning instruments.

The allusion of the title to the practice of the Grand Tour, a journey that from the 17th century engaged the "intelligences of Europe" in a pilgrimage of knowledge and culture in the Italian territories, in which Trento was also a destination, is a metaphor for the awareness of the state of the art of those geometries and natural and artificial forms that make up what we call the landscape of the city of Trento. This aerial campaign from the "View from the road" to the "view from the drone" in paraphrasing Lynch, is divided into thirteen stopovers from north to south.

Each stage is a potential milestone for surveying the environmental and urban conditions of the municipal areas, from which, over the years, it would be interesting to monitor the transformations that will take place, both environmental and anthropic.

The reason why these cornerstones were chosen and not others, involves the careful cartographic reading of the physical elements that define the landscape, described for what they are in their basic essence (Woodland Masses,

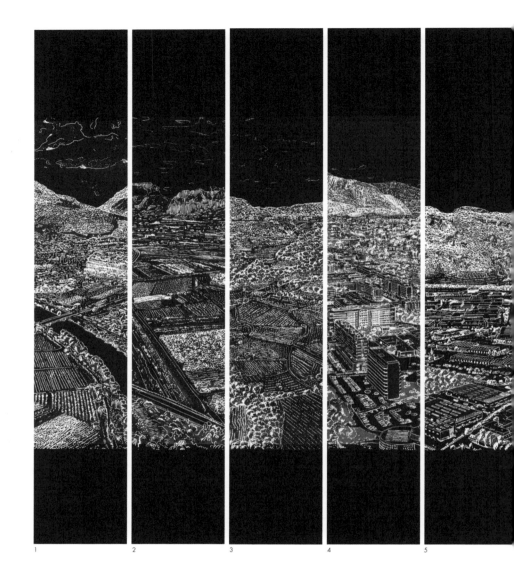

1 Riverside
2 Agricultural
3 hilltown and montain
4 Urban
5 Productive

Agricultural Textures, Adige River, Urban Textures, etc.) and in second instance for the relationships between the elements that can be encountered, described by antinomian classes, which outline multiple interactions (Built-up - Cultivated, Valley / Hillside Textures, Impermeable Soil - Permeable Soil and so on). Only later were Places, Elements and connections organised according to a scale of values, determined by their recurrence and graphically presented as word clouds, to allow an immediate reading of the components in the landscape.

The five characters

Based on the photographic description of the city, on the classification of the physical elements involved and on the relations and their interaction, a number of dominant features clearly emerge as a model of multiple natures present within the municipal context of Trento. Natures that, due to the history and stratification of the territorial palimpsest, coexist and cohabit reciprocally (Figure 6).

The close connection between recognisability and representation of the places is to be placed within the broader sphere of spatiality. Spatiality refers to the pure form of the place, determined by its location and its meaningful organisation. Physical form is fundamental for the perception and understanding of any site. Influencing the spatiality of a place implies redefining the individual components that make it up and shape it, but also paying attention to and caring for the interactions, perceptions and sensory impact that these interactions can modify. Many authors invite us to seek solutions that enhance recognisability, but also expressive languages capable of translating the intimate vocation of sites, emphasising their specific identity characteristics without sacrificing possible transformations.

The river character

The Adige, fed by its affluents in the north, draws the backbone of the valley, irrigating fields, producing energy and carrying with it road infrastructure. In the past it was an essential part of the city, now it has assumed a marginal position compared to the dynamics of the urban fabric and its interest is triggered by specific cases involving new neighbouring constructions or during particular catastrophic climatic events.

The agricultural character

The agricultural weight is considerable as it represents 20% of the entire municipal area, considering both valley and hillside plots. There are considerable differences between the northern and southern municipality boundaries, between interlocking fabrics and large plots. A landscape very much oriented towards wine monoculture, which on the one hand enhances the productive dimension, but on the other, banalises the land in its shapes and geometries.

The hill and mountain character

Half of the territory of the municipality of Trento is covered by dense woodland vegetation on the slopes of the hills surrounding the city, while the hillside, tamed by agriculture and the dusting of buildings that cover it, holds a not insignificant role in terms of urban form and the challenges associated with it, due to the urbanised continuum it produces.

The Urban Character

The geographic compression of the valley and the urban choices of the past have meant that the historic centre of the dense and compact city is now in a barycentric position in comparison to the shreds and impermeable fragments of the northern part, while the south, beyond the Fersina, shows a fringy face stretching towards agriculture that hides disused areas and places in waiting.

The Productive Character

The industrial clusters along the Via Brennero axis draw a fragmented and jagged landscape, where large, white islands of cement make the soil impermeable and sometimes trap the residential fabric. On the other hand, around the Trento South tollgate other productive situations spill over towards the city, remaining trapped in the residential fabric.

These definitions, as well as being forms of expression of the places, also seek to evolve the concept of the archipelago city, which at the time referred to the multiple identities of the urban landscape, both to carry out an operation of further synthesis and to draw frameworks in which to place the five challenges of the plan: Eco Trento, Welcoming Trento, Accessible Trento, Smart Trento, Beautiful Trento.

Sampling the voids

Open Space Structure

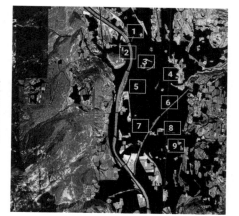

Unbuilt nature

1. Frammenti agricoli - Lavis
2. Frammenti agricoli e lacerti - Spini
3. Appezzamenti - Gardolo

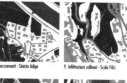

4. Tessuti agricoli interclusi - Roncafort
5. Ai margini infrastruttura - Roncafort
6. Tessuti agricoli interclusi - Melto

7. Tessuto Misto verde - Martignano
8. Appezzamenti - Sinistra Adige
9. Infiltrazioni collinari - Scalo Filzi

1. Rapporto parco / quartiere - Cristo Re
2. Frammenti verdi - Doss Trento
3. Frammenti verdi e vuoti - Piè di Castello

4. Spazi aperti e verdi - Buonconsiglio
5. Rapporto cimitero tessuti urbani - Albere
6. Frammenti verde pubblico - zona Fersina

7. Lacerti verdi - Fersina sud
8. Rapporto collina / ospedale - Bolghera
9. Schegge verdi e dismissione - San Bartolomeo

1. Tessuto agricolo intercluso - Trento frutta
2. Tessuto agricolo intercluso - Ravina
3. Tessuto agricolo intercluso - Madonna Bianca

4. Tessuti agricoli interclusi - Zona Aeroporto
5. Appezzamenti continui regolari - Martignano
6. Appezzamenti continui regolari - Aeroporto

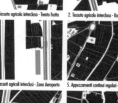

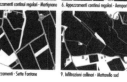

7. Limite agricolo - Mattarello
8. Appezzamenti - Sette Fontane
9. Infiltrazioni collinari - Mattarello sud

07 | Grains and Fabrics of Trento - Unbuilt Nature

Sampling the urban fabrics

Shapes of the built environment

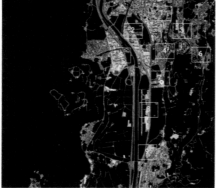

1. Grappolo di collina - Meano   2. Tessuto industriale misto - Lamar   3. Tessuto industriale - Spini ZI

4. Tessuto Residenziale - Gardolo SS12   5. Piastra Commerciale - Trento Nord   6. Tessuto Misto - Trento Nord

7. Tessuto misto - Via Brennero   8. Tessuto misto - Via Brennero   9. Filamenti collinari - Martignano

1. Tessuto residenziale misto - Cristo Re   2. Tessuto compatto - Bocconsiglia   3. Tessuto misto - Esedra stazione

4. Tessuto residenziale - Piè di Castello   5. Tessuto residenziale compatto - Centro   6. Tessuto residenziale in linea - Alb

7. Tessuto residenziale bassa densità   8. Tessuto misto e vuoti - basso Fersina   9. Tessuto misto - Santa Chiara

1. Tessuto civile e militare - Clarina   2. Tessuto industriale misto - Clarina sud   3. Tessuto collinare - Madonna Bianc

4. Tessuto misto - Madonna Bianc   5. Tessuto misto - Ravina   6. Tessuto collinare - Villazzano

7. Tessuto Industriale - Madonna B. Sud   8. Tessuto Agricolo - Aeroporto   9. Pulviscolo Residenziale - Matterello

08 | Grains and Fabrics of Trento - Built Enviroment

Space sampling

09 | Grains and Fabrics of Trento - Space Sempling

Grains and Fabrics

The previous paragraph described the landscape of the city of Trento starting from the identification of five dominant features; this part of the work, called Grains and Fabrics, instead, performs a complementary and supporting function in the understanding of the urban structure of the city through the analysis and sampling of the forms of the built environment and the shape of the open space (Figure 7, 8, 9).

The physical form of the city can be studied at different scales, depending on the extent of the parts of the city under investigation and the basic constituent elements of urban form that are being investigated. The basic structural components, either solid volumes (buildings and facilities for services) or open spaces (streets, squares, parks and gardens), are juxtaposed in the urban landscape, giving place to settlement forms that, when observed as sufficiently extended areas, may present particular characters of unity or formal homogeneity, distinguishable and classifiable on the basis of their morphological characters.

According to this principle, three urban parts plus one common to all cases have been identified, which are morphologically homogeneous in terms of grain, modularity and complexity of the settlement form. The classification is based on two macro categories of analysis, the shapes of the Built-up Environment and the Structure of the Open Space.

The first section concerns the Trento North area, the city of the large impermeable enclosures, the industrial plaques, the hard and segmented edges and the medium-sized agricultural plots enclosed by infrastructures and civil buildings. The second one, Trento Centre, is the historic and consolidated city and its porosity in terms of public space. The third one is Trento South, the open city, heterogeneous in building types and with large agricultural plots arranged in Mosaic form.

There is a fourth city, present in all three zones, with a different intensity and extent, which concerns the multiple and variegated blurred elements of the foothill and hillside fabric, created during the years by the expansion of the small towns around the city of Trento.

The three shapes were analysed at the urban scale and disaggregated according to a reading process that involves the definition of the shapes of the built-up environment and open space.

Considering that the urban tissues can be mainly classified according to two fundamental morphological characteristics: the conformation of the layout and the grain, where the layout is determined by the overall shape of the infrastructural networks, the road network, and can be distinguished as intricate, reticular, radio centric, organic and so on. The grain, on the other hand, indicates the degree of fragmentation/uniformity of the built-up texture that makes up the fabric, and is defined on the basis of the average size of the continuous building bodies in it .

The idea of the disorder of grains and the systems associated with the spatial-temporal configurations of cities has been replaced by the concept of complexity, where it is possible to treat cluttered structures as complex structures and quantify this complexity through patterns of irregularity. Based on these criteria, a mapping of grains and facilities was carried out, the study consists of a series of 54 samplings of built shapes and the structure of open space.

At the end of each mapping section there are 10 close-up shots, a hommage to the photographer Oliviero Barbieri, which show a live image of the part of the city being viewed and analysed.

Reasoned areas

The instances that emerged from the relations and elements of the Grand Tour, the features of Trento, the criticality of the urban layouts, the grains of the landscape and how they are physically encoded in the city's environment through the freeze frame of photography and interpretive diagrams, all converge in the reasoning around the five challenges proposed by the Leaf Plan. In this sense, it seemed reasonable, in order to organise the multiple activities envisaged and the different scales of action, to formulate at least four frame scenarios taking into account the criticalities of the choices made in previous plan.

Mobility infrastructures

The first issue concerns the relationship between rail and road infrastructures in relation to the surrounding area, a crucial factor for the development not only of Trento but of the entire Trentino region. The delay that the city is undergoing in facing the challenges of connectivity places many venues on hold and does not allow for both environmental and urban redevelopment of those large areas in need of new life cycles.

The crux of the problem, partly solved by the freight bypass now under tender, persists in the decision to embank part of the railway and the construction of a new train station, capable of accommodating high-speed trains, de facto downgrading the old station area.

Even the re-designing of the Scalo Filzi-Lavis axis, today nothing more than an empty space facing a totally impermeable commercial area, could be an opportunity, already discussed many times, to redevelop an entire urban flow axis in accordance with EU directives on climate change. Not only would the centre and north of Trento be touched by these transformations, but also the southern part, making it more accessible and less congested by city traf-

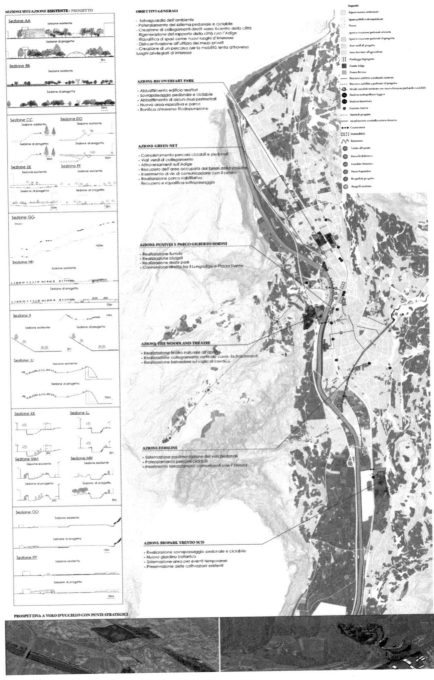

10 | Ecological and Landscape Design Experiments by Matteo Aimini and Sara Favargiotti with Silvia Mannocci and Anna Codemo during the 2019/2020 urban and architectural design workshop

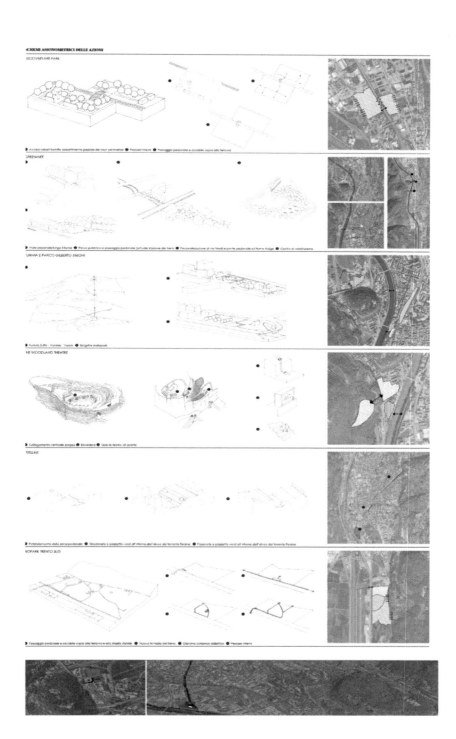

fic, and finally providing connections capable of triggering those great urban transformations, currently on hold, concerning the conversion of abandoned barracks and the definitive relocation of the hospital.

The Open Space Project

The other strategic framework concerns the themes of landscape architecture that work on a system of points (the emergencies) and lines in the territory (the pre-existences), identified in the city's existing blue and green traces (Figure 10). The places affected by these transformations are mostly disused areas (e.g. the former Italcementi quarry, now a car park, or the former SLOI chemical factory) which, with their abandonment, have developed resilient programmes of vegetation self-growth, generating real natural ecosystems to be preserved and maintained, integrating them with programs of light urban use.

For other areas now used as large car parks (former Sit and former Zuffo), there are instead plans for soil de-permeabilisation mechanisms (with draining paving) and tree planting, to mitigate heat islands; in the former Zuffo area, a new cableway station is planned to connect with Bondone and enhance the city-mountain connection.

The market streets

The other two more punctual areas of intervention concern the linear urban system of Trento Nord, the so-called 'market street', and the system of abandoned areas of Trento Sud. The first case presents a condition of considerable complexity: as envisaged by previous Plans, it was supposed to be a charming urban boulevard, but design mistakes and various malfunctions have turned it into an impassable four-lane traffic artery, surrounded by very inhomogeneous urban fabric with considerable environmental criticalities.

Modifying the road layout would also make it possible to redevelop the entire built-up area, introducing environmental mitigation devices (such as green areas at the edge of the infrastructure and in contact with the urban built-up area), actually increasing the permeability of the soil with the aid of facilities such as rain gardens and, by means of high and medium-trunk vegetation systems, restoring edge conditions now perceived only as barriers.

On the other hand, from a building point of view, especially in the compact and thinned industrial fabrics (large parts of this urban system), it would be advisable, given the morphology of the solar plexuses, to introduce roof gardens for rainwater regimentation and abatement of fine dust.

Major Strategic Areas

Trento South is facing at least three issues: the first concerns the increase in the porosity of consolidated urban fabrics, for which a selective reuse of buildings and an enlargement of draining surfaces is suggested, also through the use of low-maintenance wet gardens; the second concerns the areas of the barracks, linked to the south by a discontinuous urban fabric, interlocked between the railway and the highly congested secondary roads, for which equalization and selective thinning scenarios are suggested, in order to improve the capacity of urban systems in performance and environmental terms.

Last but not least, it concerns the "City of health" and the relocation of the entire hospital structure, today located further north in the Santa Chiara Hospital. The areas involved have a considerable index of cubic meters: they could offer a great opportunity to redesign the land and regenerate an area that is currently in a state of dormancy, but they could also offer the chance to reactivate relations with the Adige, now denied by the ring road, and with the Fersina, which has its estuary right on the border of this area.

Bibliographic references

Amin, Ash, and Stephen Graham. *The Ordinary City.* Transactions of the Institute of British Geographers, 22(4), 1997, pp. 411–429.

Barbera, Filippo, and Antonio De Rossi. *Metromontagna. Un progetto per riabitare l'Italia.* Donzelli editore, Roma, 2021.

Bonomi, Aldo, and Roberto Masiero. *Dalla smart city alla smart land.* Marsilio Editore, Venezia, 2014, pp.144

Bocchi, Renato. *Trento. Per un ritratto della città e del suo territorio nella storia e nel presente,* 2006.

Corner, James (ed.). *Recovering Landscape – Essays in Contemporary Landscape Architecture,* Princeton University Press, New York, 2013.

Curzel, Vittorio, and Beppo Toffolon. *03. "Fotografia territorio paesaggio. Quaderni del paesaggio Trentino, studi, ricerche e documentazione,* Provincia Autonoma di Trento – tsm Trentino School of Management, Trento, 2015.

Giovanazzi, Sergio, and Alessandro Franceschini (eds.). *Dossier: Bruno Kessler e il primo Pup 1961/1964, Sentieri urbani,* anno IV - numero 8. INU Trentino, 2012.

Koolhaas, Rem. *Generic City.* Published in *S,M,L,XL.* The Monacelli Press, New York, 1995.

Mioni, Alberto, Renato Bocchi, and Bruno Zanon. *Verso il nuovo piano Urbanistico. Documento programmatico,* 2000.

Zanon, Bruno. "Città a confronto – Trento". In *Il nuovo manuale di urbanistica* edited by Leonardo Benevolo and Elio Pimoddi, Mancosu Editore, Roma, 2005, pp. 46–64.

#Context

Images from the ordinary city

The "città normale"

In the grains and facilities beyond the historic centre, in the compact core that has gradually stratified itself over the centuries, where the citizenry lives on symbols, on consolidated traditions that in some ways make this condition unique and recognisable even to those who have never been there, thanks to the so-called 'iconic image effect' or 'postcard effect', other dimensions coexist. Less exceptional but just as fascinating, not so much in terms of their aesthetic nature, but rather in terms of the inevitability of their generic dimension, neglected or almost deliberately hidden.

The less noble city, built to satisfy the logic of rapid mobility, the advanced supply of services, the industrial production and the hit-and-run consumption, has been grafting itself, over the last 30 to 40 years, onto the traces of the past, breaking with the rules of the historic centre and generating a proper settling model, common to many other geographical situations in the Po Valley and the Italian peninsula, representing today, more than the historic centre, the most suffering heritage in terms of open spaces, urban infrastructures and architectural quality.

The research and narration of these liminal zones has a long and solid tradition starting with the Anti-Art of the Dada and Surrealists, with their forays into the "ordinary city" and dreamlike walkabouts to reveal the urban unconscious. Rather than Robert Smithson's urban odyssey in the industrial suburbs of Passaic, New Jersey, where the anonymous shapes of things take on a reference value and therefore a new monumental identity. The group exhibition "Journey in Italy" by a group of independent photographers including Ghirri, Basilico, Jodice and Barbieri restores the normality of a country and its everyday landscapes, breaking with the classical iconography of Italian photography that insisted on tracing the lines of the classical pictorial tradition.

Therefore, the photographic tale of the Ordinary City of Trento, in this case is not only an artistic exercise, an aimless pilgrimage, but is closely connected to the process of revising the city masterplan. The photographic campaign was anchored to a mapping of the critical zones of the agricultural and urban fabric in the plan documents. Twenty-one special zones, twenty-one surroundings to be explored, from North to South, from West to East, four months of time, a total of more than 500 shots indexed according to 26 descriptive categories (Abandonment, Enclosed Nature, Built-up Geometries, etc.). Afterwards, 70 significant shots were selected from the various categories and grouped into four families in order to form diptychs that were able to tell with forces of nature, paths, artefacts and perspectives.

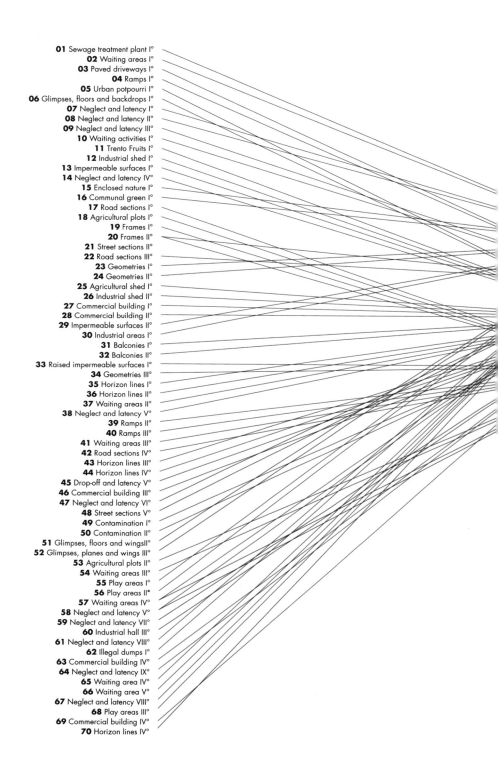

01 Sewage treatment plant I°
02 Waiting areas I°
03 Paved driveways I°
04 Ramps I°
05 Urban potpourri I°
06 Glimpses, floors and backdrops I°
07 Neglect and latency I°
08 Neglect and latency II°
09 Neglect and latency III°
10 Waiting activities I°
11 Trento Fruits I°
12 Industrial shed I°
13 Impermeable surfaces I°
14 Neglect and latency IV°
15 Enclosed nature I°
16 Communal green I°
17 Road sections I°
18 Agricultural plots I°
19 Frames I°
20 Frames II°
21 Street sections II°
22 Road sections III°
23 Geometries I°
24 Geometries II°
25 Agricultural shed I°
26 Industrial shed II°
27 Commercial building I°
28 Commercial building II°
29 Impermeable surfaces II°
30 Industrial areas I°
31 Balconies I°
32 Balconies II°
33 Raised impermeable surfaces I°
34 Geometries III°
35 Horizon lines I°
36 Horizon lines II°
37 Waiting areas II°
38 Neglect and latency V°
39 Ramps II°
40 Ramps III°
41 Waiting areas III°
42 Road sections IV°
43 Horizon lines III°
44 Horizon lines IV°
45 Drop-off and latency V°
46 Commercial building III°
47 Neglect and latency VI°
48 Street sections V°
49 Contamination I°
50 Contamination II°
51 Glimpses, floors and wingsII°
52 Glimpses, planes and wings III°
53 Agricultural plots II°
54 Waiting areas III°
55 Play areas I°
56 Play areas II°
57 Waiting areas IV°
58 Neglect and latency V°
59 Neglect and latency VII°
60 Industrial hall III°
61 Neglect and latency VIII°
62 Illegal dumps I°
63 Commercial building IV°
64 Neglect and latency IX°
65 Waiting area IV°
66 Waiting area V°
67 Neglect and latency VIII°
68 Play areas III°
69 Commercial building IV°
70 Horizon lines IV°

Categories of investigation

Nature
01 - 02 | 07 - 08 | 15 - 16 | 23 - 24 | 29 - 30 | 51 - 52 | 55 - 56 | 61 - 62 | 65 - 66 | 66 - 67

Routes
03 - 04 | 09 - 10 | 20 - 22 | 47 - 48 | 57 - 58

Fabrics
05 - 06 | 11 - 12 | 13 -14 | 25 - 26 | 27 - 28 | 31 - 32 | 35 - 36 | 37 - 38 | 43 - 44 | 45 - 46
49 - 50 | 59 - 60 | 63 - 64

Perspective
17 - 18 | 19 - 20 | 33 - 34 | 39 - 40 | 41 - 42 | 53 - 54 | 57 - 58

Fragility map and photographic survey

1° Zone
North Entrance - Via Alto Adige
Provincial level production areas in a state of underuse
Photo 07 | 64

2° Zone
Spini industrial area
Productive area of provincial level strongly conditioned by the presence of residential buildings
Photo 08

3° Zone
Spini locality
Areas subject to implementation planning
Photo 24

4t° Zone
Via Alto Adige - Intermediate section
Service area for public transport
Photo 63

5° Zone
Canova Special Project in Gardolo
Areas of the "Canova" special project subject to implementation planning
Photos 04 | 15 | 31 | 49 | 58 | 59

6° Zone
Via Bolzano North and South
C4 zone system for the formation of the "north course"
Photos 05 | 10 | 23 | 39 | 40 | 45

7° Zone
Melta Park junction
Service area for parking
Photos 13 | 17 | 20 | 25 | 35

8° Zone
Via Maccani - tertiary/directional
Areas subject to implementation planning
Photos 16 | 21 | 26 | 38 | 51 | 55 | 68

9° Zone
Campotrentino
Productive areas with widespread residential presence to be reconsidered
Photos -

10° Zone
Ex-Sloi areas - former Carbochimica
Polluted areas of Trento Nord
Photos 09 | 14 | 41 | 43 | 65

11° Zone
Via Brennero Tridente-Atesina
Areas subject to implementation planning
Photos -

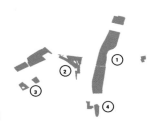

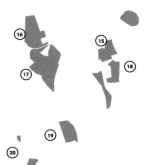

12° Zone
Scalo Filzi " Special Project - municipal property"
Urban redevelopment areas connected to the project to
bury the city section of the railway
Photos 02 | 06 | 19 | 37 | 54 | 57 | 61 | 69

13° Zone
Special Project "Stations" - Mobility Hub
Urban redevelopment areas connected to the project to
bury the city stretch of the railway
Photo -

14° Zone
Italcementi Quarry
Service area for technological installations to be
verified
Photos 47 | 62 | 64 | 67

Italcementi area
Urban void
Photo 50 | 66

15° Area
Battisti Barracks
Production areas in the PUP reserve
Photo 36

16° Zone
New Trentino Hospital NOT
Transformation area linked to the S.Chiara hospital
Photo -

17th Zone
Military areas Trento South
Military areas to be confirmed today in public green
Photo -

18° Zone
Trento Frutta redevelopment area
Urban redevelopment area
Photos 01 | 11 | 12 | 22 | 29

Former Girelli house
Existing productive areas Trento SOUTH
Photo 60

19° Zone
New production areas
Provincial-level production area
Photo 30 | 48

20° Zone
Ravina public park
Public greenery to be reconsidered
Photos 03 | 56 | 70

21° Zone
Ex-military areas
Sports area to be replanned
Photos 18 | 25

Nature

62 | Illegal dumps I - Quarry edge ex Italcementi

08 | Neglect and latency II° - Spini di Gardolo

Routes

47 | Neglect and latency VI° - Cilio di Cava - Quarry edge ex Italcementi

21 | Street sections II°° - Via Don Lorenzo Guetti

Fabrics

11 | Trento Fruits I⁰⁰ - Via Alcide DeGasperi

12 | Industrial shed I° - Via Alcide DeGasperi

Perspective

19 | Frames I° - Via Brennero

39 | Ramps II° - Via Brennero

40 | Ramps III° - Via Brennero

#Performative_tools

Ecosystem services assessment for a performance-based urban plan

Chiara Cortinovis | Davide Geneletti

This chapter, including tables and figures, is based on the article: Cortinovis, C., Geneletti, D., 2020. "A performance-based planning approach integrating supply and demand of urban ecosystem services". *Landscape and Urban Planning* 201, 103842. The full article is available open access at: https://doi.org/10.1016/j.landurbplan.2020.103842.

Introduction

As in many countries in the world, urban planning in Italy is mostly based on prescriptive zoning. A zoning plan divides the city into different zones and defines what land uses are allowed and which regulations must be respected in each zone (Janin Rivolin 2008; Frew, Baker, and Donehue 2016). This approach guarantees a high level of ex-ante control by the administration, hence a low uncertainty on the outcomes, and an easy management in the implementation phase. Proposed transformations are approved if they abide by all the rules for the respective zone. However, in the last years, the capacity of prescriptive zoning to steer territorial transformations into the outcomes desired by the community has been increasingly questioned (La Rosa and Pappalardo 2019; Ronchi, Arcidiacono, and Pogliani 2020).

Among the most criticized aspects are the so-called "standards", i.e. the minimum quantities of public services and facilities that must be provided by urban transformations depending on the expected number of new inhabitants. Originally defined as a normative tool to guarantee a minimum quality of urban transformations and a fair contribution to the needs of the community, recent critiques have focused on three main issues. First, the law (D.M. 1444/68) dates back to 1968, and the quantity defined there are not up-to-date considering the current needs of the population. Second, they are only focused on quantitative aspects, and quality, included spatial distribution, is totally overlooked. Third, they set rigid values that are applied to the entire national territory, disregarding the large variety of settlement types that can be found in Italy, and of the geographical contexts in which they are located. In the last years, several regional laws have been trying to address these issues by setting higher thresholds for the standards, or by including qualitative aspects in their assessment.

The standard related to green areas, which according to the national law sets a minimum share of 9 sqm per inhabitant to be provided by all transformations, is perhaps the most criticized. The standard, applied to small interventions and without any control on the quality of the new green spaces, has produced mostly fragmented and low-quality public green areas, somehow preventing an effective planning in terms of hierarchy and functions. Moreover, the rationale behind the standard is only focused on the provision of space for recreation, especially small pocket parks that should serve the needs of children and elderlies living close-by. Today, while we acknowledge the role of urban green spaces as suppliers of multiple ecosystem services (ES), urban planning often lacks the right tools to promote them. Standards for public and other zoning regulations for private green spaces have limited control on the features that determine the provision of many urban ES, including key regulating services such as storm-water management and micro-climate regulation.

Performance-based planning is an alternative approach to prescriptive zoning. Rather than on zones and related regulations, the primary focus of a performance-based approach is on the objectives of the plan and the desired outcomes in terms of quality of the urban environment (Baker, Sipe, and Gleeson 2006). Urban transformations are assessed against the objectives, hence approved if they contribute to meet them (Frew, Baker, and Donehue 2016). This implies a paradigm shift from rules to which transformations must conform, to levels of performance that they must reach. Where performance-based planning has been adopted, alone or in combination with prescriptive approaches, it has mostly been used to set environmental performances, among others related to air and water pollution and to storm-water management (Baker, Sipe, and Gleeson 2006). For example, instead of imposing a minimum share of permeable surface in the building lot, the plan may define requirements in terms of quality and quantity of storm-water that can be delivered to the sewage systems. Then, each developer decides how to achieve the required performance: either by limiting the building footprint and leaving a large portion of the lot unsealed, or by building more extensively but covering the buildings with green roofs, or integrating a detention basin or other technological solutions.

In this study, we developed and tested a performance-based approach that explicitly addresses the multiple ES provided by urban green spaces. More specifically, based on the assessment of the supply and demand of multiple ES, the proposed approach estimates the impacts of the urban transformations envisioned by the plan, and defines appropriate and proportionate requirements that they should meet. We describe the rationale behind the approach and the results of its testing the city of Trento, thus offering a proof-of-concept that can be further refined and adjusted to suit the specificities of different contexts.

A methodological proposal for a performance-based plan

In a performance-based approach, the process of approval of urban transformations is a process of impact assessment: a transformation is approved if, overall, it contributes to achieving the plan's objectives. Here, we use the term "urban transformations" to broadly refer to all physical interventions envisioned or allowed by a plan, not limited to land use changes (e.g., urban densification is included in the definition). To conduct the assessment, the plan identifies a set of "requirements", which allow measuring the impacts of the proposed transformations against both quantitative and qualitative objectives. The level of performance of a transformation corresponds to its capacity to positively contribute to the objectives of the plan.

Our approach moves from the consideration that urban transformations may have both positive and negative impacts on the provision of urban ES. On the one hand, urban transformations that increase soil sealing, diminish canopy coverage, or fragment valuable habitats may reduce the current supply of ES, thus negatively affecting citizens' well-being (Alberti 2005). On the other hand, urban transformations that integrate ecosystem-based actions and nature-based solutions may provide multiple benefits to the surroundings, especially in strongly urbanized areas. For example, they may contribute to water-flow regulation thus preventing urban floods (Haghighatafshar et al. 2019) or mitigate heat waves by creating cool islands (Zardo et al. 2017), thus reducing health risks associated to high temperatures (Venter, Krog, and Barton 2020).

In general, the same transformation produces at the same time both positive and negative impacts, usually on different ES (Haase et al. 2012). Hence, two broad ES-related objectives that urban transformations should pursue are: i) minimizing the negative impacts on the current ES supply, and ii) maximizing the positive impacts on the provision of ES highly demanded in the area of intervention.

Our approach combines these two objectives to ensure that the inclusion of ecosystem-based actions offsets the negative impacts generated by the urban transformation. Positive and negative impacts are not compared separately for each ES, but rather they are balanced in an overall assessment of the urban transformation, based on the principle of out-of-kind compensation. A reduction in the current supply of one ES can be compensated by an increase in the provision of other ES, provided that the latter are chosen among the most needed in the specific location where the intervention takes place. The assessment is therefore based on the analysis of both the supply and the demand of selected ES, identified as relevant to the context. The analysis of existing supply sets the basis for assessing the negative impacts of the urban transformation, while the analysis of demand is necessary to measure the positive impacts from a citizens' well-being perspective.

Within this conceptual framework, defining the performances and related requirements for urban transformations involves answering two questions:

i) what level of performance is required, i.e. how much ES supply should be provided by the urban transformation?

ii) what type of performance is required, i.e. what ES should be prioritized?

Urban ES	ES supply		ES demand		
	Indicator	Method	Intensity of hazard / level of deprivation	Population/physical assets exposed and vulnerability	Benefitting area
Microclimate regulation (cooling)	Cooling capacity of green infrastructure	Spatial modelling based on Zardo, Geneletti, Pérez-Soba, & Van Eupen (2017)	Class of cooling effect	Total population + vulnerable classes (children and elderlies)	100-m buffer
Habitat provision	Relative richness of focal species	Ecological modelling (see Pedrini, Tattoni, & Brambilla (2013) for further details)	-	-	-
Recreation	Recreation Opportunity Spectrum	Spatial modelling through ESTIMAP-recreation including input from local experts (see Cortinovis, Zulian, & Geneletti (2018) for further details)	Distance from the closest area offering high-level recreational opportunities	Total population	300-m buffer
Noise mitigation	Reduction of traffic noise at selected receivers (residential buildings)	Spatial modelling through OpeNoise QGIS plug-in (Arpa Piemonte, 2019)	Noise from roads and railroads above 65 dB	Residential buildings	Buildings potentially shielded by green barriers
Air purification	PM10 deposition	Proxy based on vegetation typology and distance from main sources	-	-	-
Runoff mitigation	Runoff avoided due to infiltration	Proxy based on the share of permeable areas	Percentage of impermeable surfaces	Total population + areas for commercial, productive, and service use	Urban sub-watershed
Food provision	Land suitability for agriculture	Proxy based on current crop typology and suitability to agricultural use	Distance from the closest community garden	Families without private garden	500-m buffer

Table 1: Methods and indicators to assess the supply and demand of the selected urban ES in Trento. More details on methods and data can be found in Cortinovis and Geneletti (2020).

In the proposed approach, the level of performance depends on the expected impact on the current ES supply: the greater the reduction in the current supply, the higher the performance that is required. The type of performance depends on the demand, i.e. on the level of priority that different ES assume in different areas of the city.

Tools to implement a performance-based approach in Trento

From an operational perspective, the implementation of the proposed approach in a planning process requires the identification of ES that are relevant to the context, and the preparation of tools that allow a rapid assessment of the expected impacts of urban transformations, hence the definition of performances and requirements. For the case study of Trento, the selection of ES was based on the strategic document approved at the beginning of the planning process, where the municipal administration defined the main goals and strategies that should steer the drafting of the new urban plan (Comune di Trento 2018). From the content analysis of the strategic document and the discussion with the municipal staff, we identified seven urban ES considered relevant for the ongoing planning process, namely micro climate regulation (cooling), habitat provision, (nature-based) recreation, noise mitigation, air purification, runoff mitigation, and food provision (Table 1).

We assessed the current supply of all the seven ES to determine the expected negative impacts of the urban transformations, hence the level of performance to require. The single ES supply maps were produced adopting various methods, from process-based models to the use of proxy, depending on data availability and resource requirements (Table 1). The assessment of demand and the definition of the type of performance, instead, was limited to five out of the seven ES mentioned in the strategic document. We excluded air purification, because ecosystem-based actions that can be implemented in the urban transformations envisioned by the plan (e.g., tree planting in new residential areas) are not expected to significantly contribute to its enhancement, and habitat provision, considering that the available data were not sufficiently detailed to capture the potential effects of small-scale interventions. The level of demand in each pixel considers both the environmental conditions (e.g., intensity of hazard) and the amount and vulnerability of population exposed within the surrounding area that could potentially benefit from the ES supplied in that pixel (Table 1).

Based on these data, we prepared two maps to support the implementation of the proposed performance-based planning approach: a "combined ES supply" map and an "integrated ES demand" map. The "combined ES

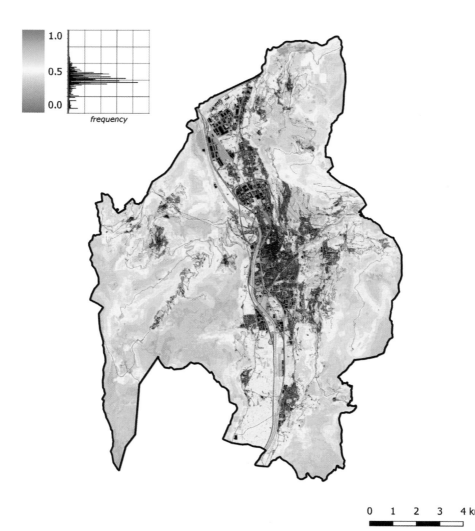

01 | Combined ES supply map

Average value of the indicator	Expected impact on ES supply	Required score (level of performance)
$0.0 \leq x < 0.2$	low	2 point
$0.2 \leq x < 0.4$	medium	4 points
$0.4 \leq x < 0.6$	high	6 points
$0.6 \leq x \leq 1.0$	very high	8 points

Table 2: Required levels of performance (score) corresponding to different classes of expected impact on the current ES supply. The classes are defined based on the average value of the indicator in the "combined ES supply" map. (See Figure 1).

supply" map synthesizes information on the supply of multiple ES and it is used to compute an overall quantitative indicator that summarizes the expected negative impacts of the urban transformation. The values in the map are obtained by summing the seven maps of ES supply rescaled to a 0-1 range and then normalizing the results. The indicator depends on the location of the urban transformation and corresponds to the overall supply of ES in the area of intervention. The quantitative values in the "combined ES supply map" are divided into classes and each class is assigned a score that represents the level of performance required to the urban transformation (Table 2).

The "integrated ES demand" map summarizes information on the demand for multiple ES across different areas of the city. It is generated by a cluster analysis based on the individual ES demand maps in order to identify areas in the city characterized by the same "demand profiles". The six clusters identified in the "integrated ES demand map" are associated to the type of performance required to the urban transformation. Depending on the location, ecosystem-based actions gain a different score based on the level of priority of the targeted ES in that cluster of demand: the higher the demand for the ES that is enhanced, the higher the score (Table 2). In this way, the most demanded ES in each area of the city are prioritized.

Through the implementation of ecosystem-based actions, each urban transformation must gain a score at least equal to the score corresponding to the required level of performance. Thus, the score serves as a link between supply and demand of multiple ES and translates the conceptual approach of balancing the impacts. The ecosystem-based actions that produce positive impacts and their minimum features in terms of size and quality should be listed in an appendix of the plan. For example, actions targeting run-off mitigation may include covering all new buildings with green roofs, or maintaining a minimum percentage of permeable surfaces in the area of intervention. The score gained by implementing these actions will depend on the level of demand for run-off mitigation where they are implemented.

Integrated ES demand map

1 | 1.37 km²
2 | 6.20 km²
3 | 115.98 km²
4 | 22.69 km²
5 | 5.35 km²
6 | 6.25 km²

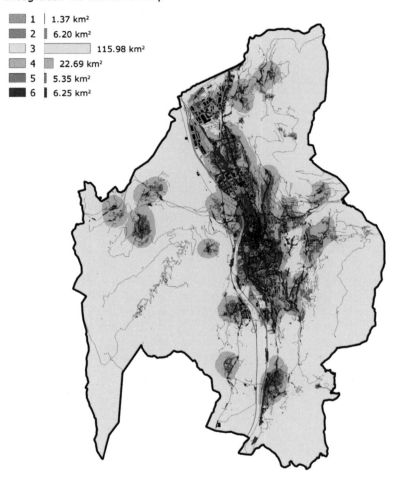

0   1   2   3   4 km

02 | Integrated ES demand map

	cluster					
	1	**2**	**3**	**4**	**5**	**6**
noise mitigation	0	0	0	0	0	4
microclimate regulation	1	1	0	1	4	3
runoff mitigation	4	4	0	0	2	2
food supply	0	1	0	2	4	3
recreation	1	2	0	1	4	3

Table 3: Scores associated to ecosystem-based actions targeting each of the five selected ES in the six clusters. Scores range from 0 to 4 and correspond to the level of demand for the specific ES in the cluster where the urban transformation is located (see Figure 2).

An exemplary application

To test the proposed approach and the scoring system, we selected two urban transformations and applied the work-flow previously described to define the level of performance and the priority ES in each case. Figure 3 shows the current state of the areas where the urban transformations are located and the respective sub-windows of the "combined ES supply" and the "integrated ES demand" maps.

The sites are two vacant lots within the most urbanized part of the city, identified as areas for in-fill development. The two sites are located in the same neighbourhood. Site A has an area of around 2,400 sqm and is currently a private garden with sparse trees, completely surrounded by developed land. Site B is a sloped terrain of approximately 1,000 sqm at the border of the built-up area and is covered by trees. The average values of the "combined ES supply" map differ between the two sites, being 0.23 for A and 0.54 for B. Accordingly, the expected impact on the current ES supply produced by the urban transformation in Site A is "medium", while the one in lot B is "high" (Table 2). The former corresponds to a required score of 4, while the latter corresponds to 6. Since both lots fall in the same cluster 5 of the "integrated ES demand" map, the priority ES to target through ecosystem-based actions are the same. The highest priority in the cluster is assigned to micro-climate regulation, food supply (urban gardens), and recreation. Actions targeting these three ES receive 4 points. A lower priority is given to runoff mitigation; therefore, actions targeting this ES receive 2 points (Table 3).

To achieve the required level of performance, urban transformation in Site A must implement at least one action aimed at strengthening one of the three priority ES in the cluster. Given the small size of the intervention, it would be difficult to implement on-site actions that enhance recreation and

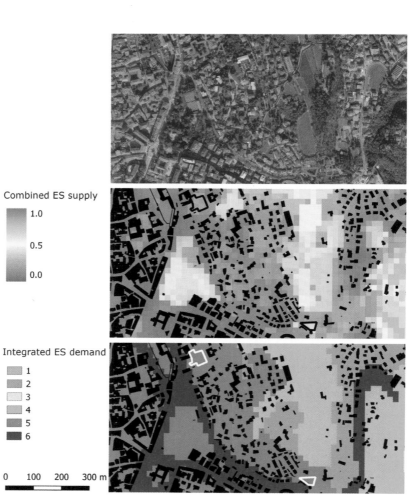

Combined ES supply

1.0

0.5

0.0

Integrated ES demand

1
2
3
4
5
6

0   100   200   300 m

03 | Combined ES supply and integrated ES demand maps of two small residential lots for in-fill development

food production. However, it is possible to maintain and increment the current tree coverage, at least in part of the area. This would guarantee a good performance of the area from the point of view of micro-climate regulation, benefiting both the future inhabitants and the surrounding residents. For the urban transformation in Site B, implementing actions to enhance micro-climate regulation would not be sufficient to achieve the required level of performance (i.e., 6 points). In this case, the intervention could also include an action targeting runoff regulation. Despite not being an absolute priority in the area, ecosystem-based actions aimed at enhancing the provision of this ES would contribute to maintain the current good condition even after the increase in the demand due to the urban transformation, thus preventing critical situations to emerge in the future.

Considerations about future applications

The performance-based approach proposed and briefly illustrated here shows some positive aspects in comparison with more traditional planning approaches. First, it shares with other performance-based approaches the capacity to define locally-specific requirements while avoiding over-prescriptive or excessively complex zoning regulations. Its ability to reflect the spatial variability of needs and values related to ES across the territory makes it a potentially more effective and more equitable tool compared to zoning, because it is more capable of answering the existing demand and counteracting the locally-specific negative impacts of the proposed urban transformations.

Another positive aspect is transparency: procedures and methods adopted to assess the impacts, as well as the requirements and related scores, are logical and reproducible. The rationale of the mechanism, i.e. balancing the negative impacts with positive contributions, is easily understandable and the maps of ES supply and demand are combined in a clear and replicable way. After the preliminary strategic stage, all the subsequent steps to build the approach are analytical and statistical procedures that do not require any decision. This reduces discretion and makes the outcomes (e.g., the scores assigned to a specific urban transformation) easy to justify and robust. The "combined ES supply" and the "integrated ES demand" maps have a simple legend and could be made available to all citizens for consultation through a web-GIS platform, thus enhancing the transparency and the legitimacy of the tool.

However, it should be noted that the ability to tailor the requirements to the expected impacts of the urban transformations and the specific needs of the surrounding area comes at the cost of complexity. The proposed approach is more complex than the other approaches under experimentation in some cities across the world, such as the Biotope Area Ratio in Berlin (Lakes and Kim 2012) or the Blue-Green- Factor in Oslo (Horvath et al. 2017; Oslo kommune 2018), and requires a higher amount of information to be processed. While an automatized generation of the maps trough a GIS software can help from the technical perspective, the administration of the process implies a different role of the public administration compared to the implementation of a zoning plan. Urban transformations are assessed within a negotiation process more complex than the simple assessment of conformity to zoning regulations. Ecosystem-based actions to increase ES provision must be assessed in their quantity with respect to the size of the area and capacity to reach the desired performance. The municipal staff must therefore acquire specific competences and face an initially steep learning curve highlighted as a limitation in previous experiences of performance-based planning (Baker, Sipe, and Gleeson 2006).

Considering its potential applicability and transferability to other contexts, one of the main strengths of the approach is its flexibility. We described an illustrative application where relevant ES have been selected based on the existing planning documents, and weighted equally to produce the synthesis maps. However, the ES can be different and weighting factors can be introduced to reflect local conditions and policy orientations about the relative importance of the different ES.

Other, non ES-based information could also be included as additional factors in the assessment process, for example as a way to differentiate the targets in different areas of the city, or to incentivize certain interventions. This flexibility ensures the adaptability of the proposed approach to different contexts and applicability beyond the single case study.

Finally, the performance-based approach must be combined with a careful preliminary assessment of where urban transformation should not be allowed at all and with appropriate tools to safeguard the provision of ES that need to be preserved. If not, there is a risk that the flexibility of performance-based planning prevents local government to halt urban development in valuable areas (Frew, Baker, and Donehue 2016). In the case of Trento, a map of ES hotspot was prepared to support the identification of valuable areas from the point of view of ES provision (Geneletti and Cortinovis 2021).

Bibliographic references

Alberti, Marina. "The Effects of Urban Patterns on Ecosystem Function." *International Regional Science Review*, vol. 28, no. 2, 2005, pp. 168–92.

Arpa Piemonte. "OpeNoise Map QGIS Plugin." 2019. https://hub.qgis.org/projects/openoise.

Comune di Trento. "Il Futuro Della Città Di Trento Si Costruisce Oggi. Obiettivi e Percorso Della Variante Generale Al Piano Regolatore Generale. / The Future of the City of Trento Is Being Built Today. Objectives and Process of the Overall Revision to the Urban Plan." Trento, 2018. https://www.comune.trento.it/Aree-tematiche/Ambiente-e-territorio/Urbanistica/Il-nuovo-PRG-Piano-regolatore-generale/Obiettivi-e-percorso-della-variante-generale-al-Piano-regolatore-generale-2018/Scarica-il-documento-Il-futuro-della-citta-di-Trento-si-cos.

Cortinovis, Chiara, and Davide Geneletti. "A Performance-Based Planning Approach Integrating Supply and Demand of Urban Ecosystem Services." *Landscape and Urban Planning*, vol. 201, 2020, p. 103842.

Cortinovis, Chiara, Grazia Zulian, and Davide Geneletti. "Assessing Nature-Based Recreation to Support Urban Green Infrastructure Planning in Trento (Italy)." *Land*, vol. 7, no. 4, 2018, p. 112.

Frew, Travis, Douglas C. Baker, and Paul Donehue. "Performance Based Planning in Queensland: A Case of Unintended Plan-Making Outcomes." *Land Use Policy*, vol. 50, 2016, pp. 239–51.

Geneletti, Davide, and Chiara Cortinovis. "Identifying Ecosystem Service Hotspots to Support Urban Planning in Trento." In *Ecosystem Services and Green*

Infrastructure. Cities and Nature, edited by Andrea Arcidiacono and Silvia Ronchi. Cham: Springer, 2021.

Haase, Dagmar, Nina Schwarz, Michael W. Strohbach, Franziska Kroll, and Ralf Seppelt. "Synergies, Trade-Offs, and Losses of Ecosystem Services in Urban Regions: An Integrated Multiscale Framework Applied to the Leipzig-Halle Region, Germany." *Ecology and Society*, vol. 17, no. 3, 2012, p. 22.

Haghighatafshar, Salar, Mikael Yamanee-Nolin, Anders Klinting, Maria Roldin, Lars-Göran Gustafsson, Henrik Aspegren, and Karin Jönsson. 2019. "Hydroeconomic Optimization of Mesoscale Blue-Green Stormwater Systems at the City Level." *Journal of Hydrology*, vol. 578, September 2019, p. 124125.

Horvath, Peter, David N. Barton, Espen Aukrust, Hauglin Halvor, and Weider Ellefsen. 2017. "Blue-Green Factor (BGF) Mapping in QGIS User Guide and Documentation." 1445. NINA Report. Oslo. https://www.nina.no/Portals/NINA/Bilder og dokumenter/Prosjekter/Urban EEA/NINA Report 1445 - BGF in QGIS.pdf.

Lakes, Tobia, and Hyun Ok Kim. "The Urban Environmental Indicator 'Biotope Area Ratio' - An Enhanced Approach to Assess and Manage the Urban Ecosystem Services Using High Resolution Remote-Sensing." *Ecological Indicators*, vol. 13, no. 1, 2012, pp. 93–103.

La Rosa, Daniele, and Viviana Pappalardo. "Planning for Spatial Equity - A Performance Based Approach for Sustainable Urban Drainage Systems." *Sustainable Cities and Society*, October 2019, p. 101885.

Oslo kommune. "Brukerveiledning for Blågrønn Faktor i Boligprosjekter i Oslo." 2018. https://www.oslo.kommune.no/getfile.php/13298013/Innhold/Plan%2C bygg og eiendom/Byggesaksveiledere%2C normer og skjemaer/Blågrønn faktor - Brukerveiledning for blågrønn faktor.pdf.

Pedrini, Paolo, Clara Tattoni, and Mattia Brambilla. "Individuazione Della Connettivitá e Della Frammentazione Ecologica a Livello Provinciale e Verso i Territori Limitrofi." Trento. 2013. http://www.lifeten.tn.it/binary/pat_lifeten/azioni_preparatorie/LifeTEN_Report_A3.1395234092.pdf.

Janin Rivolin, Umberto. "Conforming and Performing Planning Systems in Europe: An Unbearable Cohabitation." *Planning Practice and Research*, vol. 23, no. 2, 2008, pp. 167–86.

Ronchi, Silvia, Andrea Arcidiacono, and Laura Pogliani. "Integrating Green Infrastructure into Spatial Planning Regulations to Improve the Performance of Urban Ecosystems. Insights from an Italian Case Study." *Sustainable Cities and Society*, vol. 53, February 2020, p. 101907.

Venter, Zander S., Norun Hjertager Krog, and David N. Barton. "Linking Green Infrastructure to Urban Heat and Human Health Risk Mitigation in Oslo, Norway." *Science of the Total Environment*, vol. 709, 2020, p. 136193.

Zardo, Linda, Davide Geneletti, Marta Pérez-Soba, and Michiel van Eupen. "Estimating the Cooling Capacity of Green Infrastructures to Support Urban Planning." *Ecosystem Services*, vol. 26, 2017, pp. 225–35.

#Performative_tools

Collaborative urban plan as driver of changing

Francesca Marzetti

Adaptive urban planning

The contemporary city is a complex organism, in which the social, economic, environmental, and technological context changes constantly. Public administrations human and economic availability resources are increasingly limited, citizenship has acquired an essential proactive, role in urban processes and contractors see less demand from the real-estate market and available capital. The climate change effects are tangible in our daily lives and the pandemic is causing a health, social and economic crisis. Conventional urban planning tools have failed to respond to city changes due to the rigidity of systems, regulations, and procedures and have remained anchored in a spatial prefiguration of a city in medium-long term.

In this framework, the collaborative urban transformation processes can support the new adaptive urban plan, going beyond the traditionally opposition relationship between strategies and tactics and replacing conventional zoning, sectoral, linear, and typological schemes with the exchange of relationships between interconnected and non-predefined networks, where there are temporary solutions (Branzi 2010).

The institutional experiences aimed at introducing and testing flexible processes in terms of times, uses, and procedures symbolize their new awareness of the need to stress conventional urban planning devices. On the other hand, the phenomenon of spontaneous tactical urbanism was created in the 1970s to fill in the gaps in traditional urban planning tools. In bottom-up urban tactics, citizens are the main actors in re-appropriating and reactivating social urban space through quick, easy, and feasible interventions that are low cost, provisional, changeable, and daily (Lydon and Garcia 2015). Since tactical actions are not stable, they have not been considered by conventional urban planning tools and were often realized without the necessary authorization.

The relationship between the two approaches was marked by a gradual shift from disagreement to collaboration through a transition period in which public administrations tested and then supported urban tactics.

The metabolic (Wolman 1965), adaptive (Rauws and De Roo 2016), open (Gausa 2010) urban plan, like the Trento Leaf Plan, is the combination of challenges that change over time and are detailed according to different needs. The new urban plan can adapt to different and unexpected situations evolving from a qualitative and not quantitative point of view. It is not a conventional general urban plan, but a vision of the city and related networks implemented in stages and with different tools that looks at the present by interpreting the city's needs and resources (Girot 2006; Guallart 2013).

Collaborative urban transformations in Space, Time and Sense of Belongings

These urban transformations (projects, programmes, and actions) succeed at addressing the city challenges quickly and decisively, step by step. City strategies can no longer coincide with an urban planning tool, political agenda, or a mission statement, but is rather a plural vision and method that arises through multi-scalar, innovative practices capable of making policies work synergistically.

The Cobe studio's project to redevelop the Norreport Station in Copenhagen in 2015 following a design competition is an example of such an approach in which, according to the studio, "form follows people". The project transforms the concept of the railway station from a place for waiting and transferring, into a partially covered square that follows the continuous flows and routes that change with the passage of time and the seasons – flows studied by the designers through the traces left by users on the snow in winter. The area has gone from being a dangerous crossroads to a meeting place, where parking spaces for bicycles are built into depressions in the ground to make them recognizable, reducing its visual impact and, in extreme weather events, acting as rainwater containment area.

The collaboration also concerns the actors involved in city changes. Public administrations and designers take a less authoritative stance by also empowering citizens, associations, designers, and economic enterprises with whom they share the city vision and the practices capable of implementing and stimulating them.

The new form of collaboration between strategic and tactical behaviour finds space in the topics "Space, Time, and Sense of belonging", which, in different ways and with different weights, are related to each other and present in all the different experiences examined.

Space is the manifestation of a new idea of public place that aims for performance rather than quantity, overcoming zoning by favouring multifunctionality and changes in use, disregarding the proprietary nature of goods and services. Traditional planning attempts to find a balance, to determine the city and space through control, pre-definition and the definition of boundaries to divide different entities. On the contrary it is composed of porous membranes of exchange and borders along which different entities interact and stimulate each other (Sennet 2007). Traditional urban planning strives for balance, while

01 | Norreport Station, Cobe. Citizens' flows. Photo © Rasmus Hjortshøj - COAST

the open city as an organism is incomplete and characterized by "conflict and dissonance" (Sennet 2006).

The digital revolution has contributed to changing the value of time and the related concept of physical space (Bauman 2011; Ratti 2017). The time and space needed to live, work, and interact have become increasingly shorter, sometimes shifted to the Internet, sometimes leading to the emptying of functional containers and the obsolescence of the road system. It is therefore no longer time to expand physical urban space and networks, but rather work on the quality and regenerate what exists. Accessibility, technological suitability, environmental, social, and economic sustainability, reversibility, maintainability of public spaces, sharing of design and implementation process, and support for services provided by private entities, are just some of the qualitative characteristics of public and private space.

Public space is a vital element of the city and for it to fulfil its function, multi-scale projects, small scale changes, citizen involvement, and a multitude of uses that complement and support each other economically and socially must be favoured (Jacobs 2000).

Liveability and spatial quality are relative concepts, but they are always the result of a process that considers perception and relationships and not a design that measures distances and marks boundaries (Gehl 2010). The new concept of space rejects the pretence of top-down city design and welcomes an increasingly clear spontaneous and flexible component that actively adapts to the changes in the city and its citizens. When necessary, the action of citizens who experience the space is capable of modifying its nature, use, function, and import that is predetermined and derives from a top-down design.

In this context, the in-between spaces are not necessary a void, the space left between the other urban elements, but can be a place of interest, a hinge, a network that connects (Gausa 2003) relationships and parts of the consolidated city. The experiences Groundplay in San Francisco and the ex Officine Reggiane in Reggio Emilia show how these residual areas can become resources as well as the Superillas in Barcelona and Piazze Aperte in Milano demonstrate how even spaces intended for vehicular mobility can be questioned and given back to citizens.

Time represents the new urban vision composed of complex challenges. It is implemented in steps and no longer through general modifications to the general plan and the long-term strategic vision gives way to the everyday life of the city. Just as the long term was the symbol and operating principle of solid modernity, the short term is the reference for fluid modernity, based on the instantaneousness (Bauman 2011). Time goes on two speeds: the accelerated speed of technology that influences our life, social relations, communication and the *lungo presente* where conventional spaces change slowly, and they seem devoid of meaning (Ricci 2019).

In this context, urban tactics are a tool for contributing to change through their ability to listen and survive to it; their collaboration with strategies ensures that they do not remain isolated experiences but can be considered as part of the new collaborative approach to the city. The temporary nature of the interventions actively adapts to changing external conditions and thus manages to create the basis for improving the quality of life today without claiming to anticipate the future, as evidenced by the experiences of the Stalled Spaces in Glasgow, and the *Pla BUITS* in Barcelona. The *Delibera degli Indirizzi per gli usi temporanei* in Napoli rehabilitate large public buildings for social purposes by giving meaning to it and improving its performances (ibid.).

The desire to respond to the city needs today without postponing them to some future time does not mean limiting the field by disregarding the consequences of short-term actions and interventions. On the contrary, this approach consciously proposes and experiments with actions and interventions that trigger processes that will inevitably influence the future (Ratti 2017). The collaboration between tactics and strategies is intended to enable the future, not to govern it; in contrast, traditional urban planners quantify, design, and regulate urban transformations by predicting future scenarios often without considering the (ten-year plus) time between planning and implementation. It is therefore necessary to use systems that are open to change over time, allowing for overlapping and indeterminacy, for example, of uses over time. These are reversible interventions that represent a new approach capable of dialoguing with places and users in a more flexible, informal, and dynamic way and adapting to the temporary nature and contingency of events (Gausa 2003). In this sense, interim uses are developed pending the implementation of regular stable interventions or to reactivate major urban regeneration projects. Such is the experience of the *Darsena* in the City of Ravenna, in which the rigidity of urban planning tools is overcome in terms of both procedures and urban forecasts, compensating for the inability of the plans to facilitate implementation of the expected projects.

Sense of belonging is understood as the social function of urban transformation experiences that follow changes in urban behaviour and respond to new social habitats in the city.

Contemporary communities no longer identify with the use of traditional public space designed by designers and implemented by public administrations.

Henry Lefebvre's "right to the city", understood as the right to urban life and social places (1970), is replicated by Harvey as the collective right "to change and to reinvent the city" (2012). In this context, democracy is understood not in its strictest sense as the legal and regulatory apparatus that allows for a state of legality, but as a physical experience that focuses on community and shared experiences. The participatory processes accompanying top-down design and planning have been replaced by shared experiences, such as the

02 | Bang, Ai Weiwei, German Pavillon, 55 Art Exhibition Biennale di Venezia, 2013.
Photo by Simone Anzini

Arquitectos de Cabecera in Barcelona. As such, citizens are not only considered as the final beneficiaries of a project or planning forecasts, or as voters to please, but as real collaborators to be relied on in the planning, management, and implementation phases. Citizens no longer passively submit to and consume what is imposed from above but are self-aware and are determined to pragmatically and quickly resolve everyday issues. They are prosumers (Toffler, 1980), that is, producer-consumers, described by Anna Meroni as citizens who, thanks to in-depth knowledge of local situations, are aware and become the most suitable subjects for finding effective solutions for the public space which would otherwise risk remaining like hardware without software (2007). In accord with Lucius Burckhardt (2019), traditional planning did not often address the question of how citizens saw and experienced the city, how they perceived the realization of politicians' wishes and solutions translated by designers into neighbourhoods, buildings, and infrastructure. His "self-fulfilling prophecies" typical of traditional urban planning solve individual problems in the city but fail to improve the quality of life. The experience in Zaragoza with *Estononesunsolar* and the one in Napoli with the *Fondazione Quartieri Spagnoli – FOQUS* illustrate how it is no longer possible to rely only on public resources (in terms of both skills and money) and how it is time.

to find and experiment with new forms of cooperation and collaboration between the public and private sectors and cooperation between companies.

For a public space to function, in the sense that it be used by citizens, it is essential that they spontaneously infuse it with a social function (Burckhardt 2019), recognizing it as a place of reference for interaction and exchange. The "trust on a public street" is also indispensable for nurturing citizens' sense of belonging and it is a characteristic that is gained spontaneously by establishing contacts and close relationships and cannot be obtained in a pre-defined and planned way (Jacobs 2000).

Administrators and planners cannot define and design spaces that draw on the sphere of sociality and everyday life and think that these spaces will be successful; they can, however, act as facilitators and enablers of the social functions of public space, as the experience of *Spazi in movimento* in Rovereto shows.

An Open Toolbox for Collaborative Urban Transformations

The The Open Toolbox proposal does not want to definitively respond to the needs of the city, but that can be considered as a framework to which the municipality can refer in a different time to respond to various needs (economic, social, environmental, administrative). This is an operational reference based on which it is possible to work within an overall vision that is able to give concrete and verifiable answers in certain and short times. From the three topics of

"Time, Space and Sense of belonging" that span the five challenges, emerging strategies, tactics, and devices were therefore identified.

The 6 strategies proposed are united by their commitment to encouraging spontaneous action in order to anticipate citizens' needs and understand their requirements, nurture a plurality of visions, and encourage intercultural integration.

– Performance (vs zoning and standards), which favours multifunctionality and changes in use over time, the performance of interventions over a quantitative approach to public spaces and facilities.

– No net land take (vs building development), for a zero-land-use plan capable of minimizing waste by reusing what exists, regenerating rather than replacing buildings or expanding city.

– Urban tactics (vs urban planning), to create spaces that improve the quality of life in a quick, adaptable and experimental way, moving from the decade-long dimension of traditional tools to the day-to-day dimension of tactical urbanism.

– Projects (vs urban transformation plans), to favour the feasibility of interventions through an implementable and flexible plan instead of designs for new parts of the city and regulations for large urban transformations.

– Sharing (vs participation), for active collaboration between the different actors involved in the entire urban transformation process (from conception to maintenance) and going beyond the simple communication of choices already organized for acquiring the consent of citizens.

– Cooperation (vs welfarism), to act jointly by sharing responsibilities and resources, and to increase knowledge and expertise by contributing experiences and cultures, overcoming a self-referenced approach that is based more on assistance than on exchange.

Starting from these strategies, 10 tactics were identified as a way to organize processes and mechanisms to face challenges. These mechanisms can be modified and implemented and can respond to the needs of different actors, working on different scales and stages (procedural management, implementation and maintenance):

– General plan amendment, thematic and specific modifications to address the challenges, goals, and actions in a flexible way that can be implemented over time.

– Adaptive plan open platform, through which citizens can request information and present proposals to implement and adapt the plan. Proposals could be evaluated on a medium-term basis (e.g. every two years) by a technical group to update the goals and actions.

– Chief resilience officer, an expert who works with a municipal operations unit to create a network and systematize the city's various initiatives and programmes, also coordinating the municipal offices concerned and the bodies involved in the procedures.

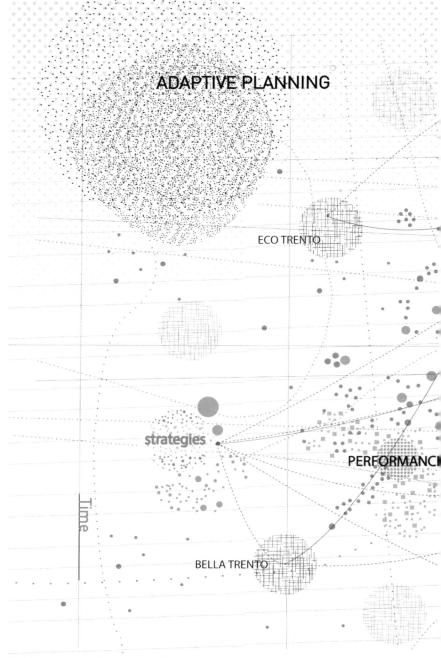

ADAPTIVE PLANNING

ECO TRENTO

strategies

PERFORMANC

Time

BELLA TRENTO

03 | Adaptive planning in Trento; concept Francesca Marzetti, graphic elaboration Francesca Malecore

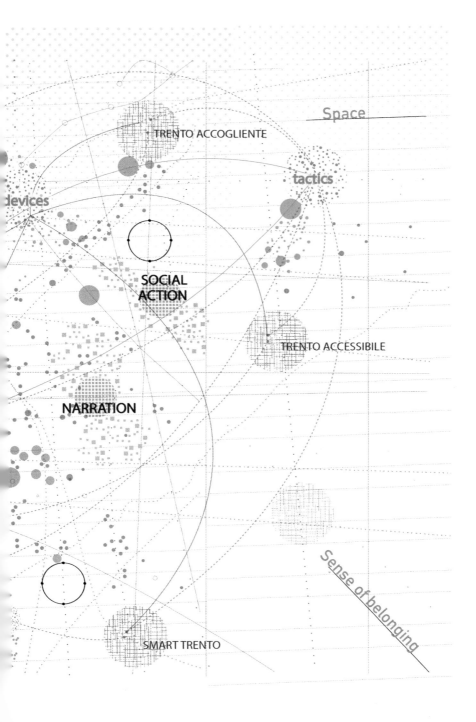

Space

TRENTO ACCOGLIENTE

tactics

devices

SOCIAL
ACTION

TRENTO ACCESSIBILE

NARRATION

Sense of belonging

SMART TRENTO

139

04 | An Open Toolbox for Collaborative urban Transformations; concept Francesca Marzetti, graphic elaboration Francesca Malecore

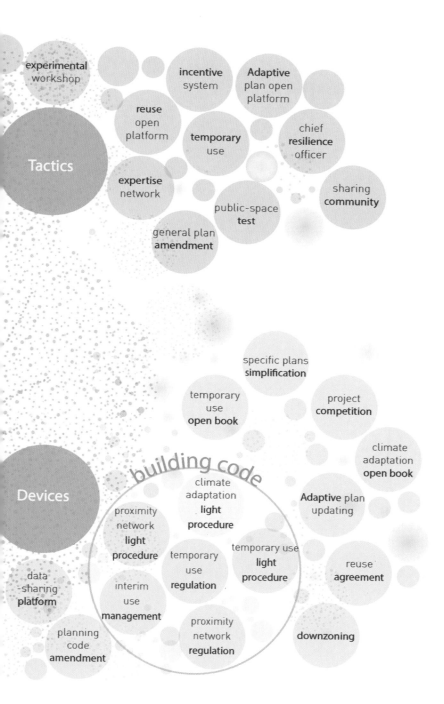

experimental
workshop

incentive
system

Adaptive
plan open
platform

reuse
open
platform

temporary
use

chief
resilience
officer

Tactics

expertise
network

sharing
community

public-space
test

general plan
amendment

specific plans
simplification

temporary
use
open book

project
competition

climate
adaptation
open book

building code

climate
adaptation
light
procedure

Adaptive plan
updating

Devices

proximity
network
light
procedure

temporary
use
regulation

temporary use
light
procedure

reuse
agreement

data
-sharing
platform

interim
use
management

proximity
network
regulation

downzoning

planning
code
amendment

The goal is to identify a fast and simple authorization process upstream that is flexible so it can meet not only the needs of citizens and economic activities, but also ensure respect for the city's landscape and cultural values.

– Sharing community, in the form of organizing services in flat complexes or neighbourhood (assistance, cultural and expertise exchange through the working time accounts) and hospitality (young people-seniors), encouraged through tax relief and/or simplification of authorization procedures for collective use of the premises.

– Experimental workshop, where the administration, citizens, universities, businesses, and associations can share spaces and experiences to reactivate the socioeconomic circumstances of areas/factories and rediscover the importance of the neighbourhood, multiculturalism, innovation, and reuse, each making their experience, skills, and tools available to others; to create a network and cultural base and propose projects.

– Reuse open platform, to encourage the reuse of existing heritage. Citizens will be able to offer suggestions, ask for information, and establish contacts. The public administrations and associations will be able to provide assistance with and information about different opportunities1 (location, demand supply, technical and administrative assistance), procedures, and possible levels of intervention.

– Expertise network, a sharing of processes and information between public, private, research, and university entities for work on two levels. One level for defining the paths to be followed and a more operational level of collaboration2 to exchange information and expertise to address the challenges in a multidisciplinary way. Participation in cooperation programmes, workshops, and seminars, implementation of direct relationships between public administrations for continuous updating and discussion with other institutions and administrations, are some of the possible occasions of exchange of views and experiences.

– Incentive system, that rewards virtuous behaviour3 through local tax relief (abatement of property taxes, household utilities, discount system) and/or simplified procedures, and discourages behaviour that is inconsistent with the challenges of the plan (e.g. city taxes for empty buildings or unused areas, parking tariff system that encourages transfers with slow mobility).

– Public-space test of possible solutions for collective spaces by reducing roadways in favour of biking/pedestrian areas, but also testing new uses to reactivate spaces for socialization and multiculturalism.

– Temporary use of spaces, functions, and buildings for public and private use in small ordinary interventions and in areas to be regenerated, also providing for small interventions and implementation in steps.

The strategies and tactics can be implemented through 15 devices, as flexible tools that can be modified and adapted over time, according to different needs:

downzoning, to downgrade building plots to adapt the plan to new city and citizen's needs; specific plans simplification, in terms of ownership, destination, and uses to facilitate the regeneration of complex areas demanding detailed planning; planning code amendment, specific regulatory modifications of the urban plan to simplify the feasibility and encourage the implementation of interventions; reuse agreement, for unused or underused areas or to enhance to favour sharing processes, simplify the management of public spaces, and stimulate the reuse of existing ones; project competition to regenerate, reactivate, and organize the different areas of the city and for projects and services regarding mobility; incrementable data sharing platform to share information, experiences, proposals, and projects; creation and on-line publication of the temporary use open book and the climate change adaptation open book to share knowledge, designs, tests, and implementation of interventions.

Through the periodic adaptive plan update, the necessary adjustments will be made on three levels: the first concerns the updating (detail/modification) of the actions already planned (e.g. projects, agreements with other institutions and relationships with sector plans); the second concerns the adjustments of the urban planning tools (e.g. plans not implemented, verification of the implementation status of major projects); the third concern the introduction of new actions necessary to reach the goals.

The new national building code model plays a key role as a useful tool to face the challenges and could be therefore implemented at local level through: interim use management in complex areas, also useful for reactivating the urban transformation processes established by the related detailed plans; temporary use regulation in ordinary development areas to supply citizens with quick answers and also facilitate projects for reuse rather than replacement, to simplify the interventions and answer the need for flexibility and adaptability; the proximity network regulation to incentivize and simplify activities for sharing services and structures, limiting as much as possible car usage and reactivating the sense of belonging in the neighbourhood community; the definition of light procedure to facilitate and encourage projects for temporary use, proximity networks, and climate change adaptation, speeding up the issuing of permits, avoid the overlapped procedures (also through the establishment of a steering committee), making the rules coherent with the incentives and more flexible.

The proposed strategies, tactics and devices are not sector-based but work together and address more than one of the challenges and their details. The choice was made to propose an Open Toolbox that can be calibrated and modified over time.

The Open Toolbox was tested into the Trento Leaf Plan to verify if and how it can help to implement the new urban plan connecting 6 strategies with the 5 challenges, the 10 tactics with the 15 goals, and the 15 devices with the 61 actions.

Manifesto for Adaptive Planning

In the Manifesto for Adaptive Planning is summarized the new planning approach proposed for the Trento Leaf Plan by the TUT group.

1. ECO
1.1 - Zero volumes, for an urban plan that does not increase land consumption and that encourages the recovery of waterproofed soils and the reuse of the existing one.

1.2 - Climate change Adaptation, for a more liveable city capable of adapting to climate change at different scales: from the building to the neighbourhood, to infrastructures and public works.

1.3 - Open territory, to catalyse attention on natural and agricultural open spaces that are increasingly multifunctional and connected to the urban reality in terms of relationships, production, and resources.

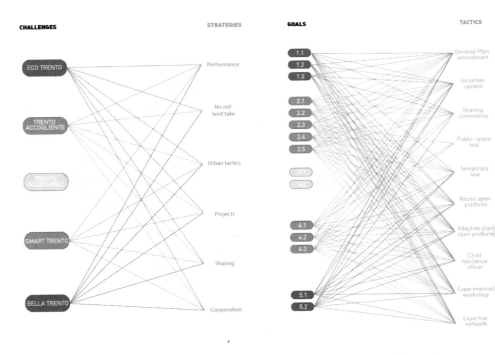

05 | Testing the Open Toolbox on the Trento Leaf Plan; concept Francesca Marzetti, graphic elaboration Francesca Malecore

2. ACCOGLIENTE

2.1 - Urban recycling, to support the regeneration and reuse of the existing, making it possible not to waste resources, to reactivate the sense of belonging and cooperation between the various actors involved in urban transformations.

2.2 - Housing polices, to sustain disadvantaged categories but also to strengthen collaboration between citizens, by sharing services and spaces.

2.3 - Flexibility, to facilitate the implementation of interventions, monitoring the needs of the territory which are constantly changing and calibrating the related tools and devices.

2.4 - Service network, to make the best use of existing resources that provide services to the community and improve their performance, updating the heritage of services to meet the new needs of citizens, encouraging cooperation and reuse.

2.5 Attractiveness, to reactivate/activate the ability to attract tourists through the diversification of the offer, the services offered, accessibility, improving the attractiveness of the city.

3. ACCESSIBILE

3.1 - Mobility hub, to improve accessibility and encourage the use of public transport, including through the upgrading of equipment and related services.

3.2 - Mobility network, to improve the integrated management of services, encouraging networking and inter-modality of transport and multidisciplinary planning.

4. SMART

4.1 - Connection, to support a network of relationships (e.g. research bodies, innovative companies and the third sector realities) and to create enabling facilities network (material and immaterial) for companies and public sector.

4.2 - Reconversion, to encourage business versatility monitoring the implementation of the urban plan and facilitating temporary use and the flexibility of uses permitted.

4.3 - Feasibility, to facilitate and speed up the times of urban transformations and to reactivate regeneration interventions.

4.4 - Simplification, to encourage the activation and implementation of transformations and make the urban planning tool efficient and its management collaborative.

4.5 - Zero energy, for a city with zero balance energy consumption. To respond to the climate change effect, with regard to support technologies and integration processes between adaptation and mitigation measures.

5. BELLA

5.1 Enhancing Landscape, as an element of reconnection between the urban and natural environments and an indispensable resource for the metabolic and adaptive plan.

5.2 Reactivating the cultural and architectural Heritage to improve the quality of life by highlighting the link between buildings and historic centres with the contemporary city; considering them not only as assets to be protected, but also as resources to be experienced and enhanced.

The eight actions proposed for the Manifesto are cross cutting, contribute to reaching all the goals in different ways and can be implemented through the Open Toolbox devices. For this reason, in the Manifesto we find the most significant actions for each challenge associated with the devices capable of activating them. The actions will be more detailed in the different application experiences, as was done in the Leaf Plan.

Improving performance: interventions that enhance the performance of urban transformations in terms of environment and energies, material/intangible connections, adequacy of urban planning tools, ability to make the city welcoming and attractive and the use of services and landscape and architectural heritage.

Enabling Urban regeneration: it concerns interventions that redevelop the existing city also allowing to improve the sense of belonging, social relations, and the attractiveness of the city, also on the environmental aspect.

Rewards for worthy behaviour: to encourage or discourage those that are in contrast with the challenges and goals of the urban plan. They mainly concern the theme of adaptation and mitigation of climate change (building retrofitting, disincentivising of private transport) and the enhancement of cultural-architectural heritage.

Monitoring territorial dynamics: to understand how the trends and needs of citizens change and then respond quickly through rapid and flexible interventions and tools. They concern the mechanisms and devices to support monitoring, such as the census of the interventions to be reactivated/incentivized and that of the properties to be enhanced. But it is also useful for updating the urban plan by calling citizens to submit proposals on predefined topics (e.g. downgrading, simplification of implementation plans).

Supporting PPP: to facilitate the feasibility, management and maintenance of interventions concerning urban transformation processes and the realization and provision of services.

Co-design: to reactivate collaboration processes between public administration and citizens, private individuals, companies, and research bodies, to understand, test and rapidly implement responses to citizens' needs.

Communication: to connect the various actors involved in urban transformations, share initiatives, information, needs and knowledge. But also, to create a direct communication channel between public bodies and the actors of urban transformations to compare points of view and needs and then identify solutions.

Simplification: to incentivize the feasibility of interventions and the activation of initiatives through the simplification of procedures and the collaboration between the bodies involved to encourage the achievement of related goals.

These actions – catalysed by the Open Toolbox devices and through the Collaborative urban Transformations – activate the ecological transition: an adaptive, multi-scalar and interdisciplinary process that leads towards a city more ECO, ACCOGLIENTE, ACCESSIBILE, SMART and BELLA.

COLLABORATIVE URBAN TRANSFORMATION - A Manifesto for adaptive planning

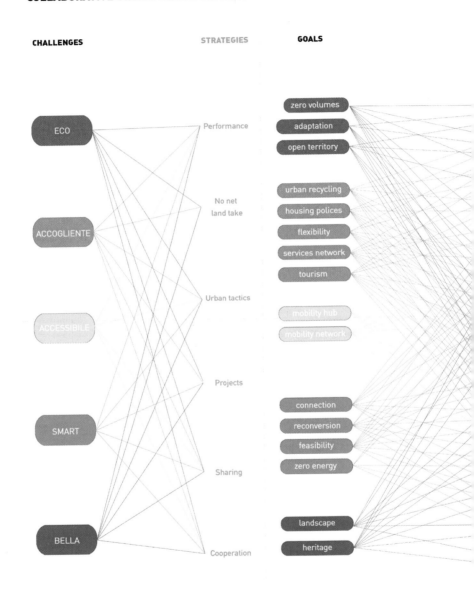

06 | Manifesto for adaptive planning; concept Francesca Marzetti,
graphic elaboration Francesca Malecore

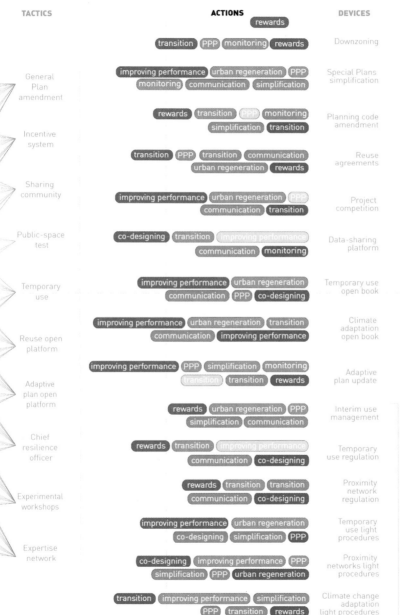

TACTICS

General Plan amendment

Incentive system

Sharing community

Public-space test

Temporary use

Reuse open platform

Adaptive plan open platform

Chief resilience officer

Experimental workshops

Expertise network

ACTIONS

rewards

transition   PPP   monitoring   rewards

improving performance   urban regeneration   PPP
monitoring   communication   simplification

rewards   transition   PPP   monitoring
simplification   transition

transition   PPP   transition   communication
urban regeneration   rewards

improving performance   urban regeneration   PPP
communication   transition

co-designing   transition   improving performance
communication   monitoring

improving performance   urban regeneration
communication   PPP   co-designing

improving performance   urban regeneration   transition
communication   improving performance

improving performance   PPP   simplification   monitoring
transition   transition   rewards

rewards   urban regeneration   PPP
simplification   communication

rewards   transition   improving performance
communication   co-designing

rewards   transition   transition
communication   co-designing

improving performance   urban regeneration
co-designing   simplification   PPP

co-designing   improving performance   PPP
simplification   PPP   urban regeneration

transition   improving performance   simplification
PPP   transition   rewards

DEVICES

Downzoning

Special Plans simplification

Planning code amendment

Reuse agreements

Project competition

Data-sharing platform

Temporary use open book

Climate adaptation open book

Adaptive plan update

Interim use management

Temporary use regulation

Proximity network regulation

Temporary use light procedures

Proximity networks light procedures

Climate change adaptation light procedures

BUILDING CODE

Bibliographic references

Arena, Gregorio, and Christian Iaione. *L'età della condivisione. La collaborazione fra cittadini e amministrazioni per i beni comuni.* Carocci, 2015.

Bauman, Zygmunt. *La società dell'incertezza.* Translated by Roberto Marchisio and Savina Neirotti. Il Mulino, 1999.

Bauman, Zygmunt. *Modernità liquida.* Translated by Sergio Minnucci. Laterza, 2011.

Branzi, Andrea. "For a Post-Environmentalism: seven suggestions for a new Athens charter". In *Ecological Urbanism,* edited by Mohsen Mostafavi and Gareth Doherty, pp. 12-13. Lars Müller Publishers, 2010.

Burckhardt, Lucius. "Design per il quotidiano". In *Il falso è l'autentico,* edited by Gaetano Licata and Martin Schmitz. Translated by Carla Buttazzi and Elisa Ricci, pp. 99-106. Quodlibet Habitat, 2019.

Cobe - Norreport Station. (n.d.). https://www.cobe.dk/ place/norreport-station [accessed 20.11.2020].

Gehl, Jan. *Cities for People.* Island Press, 2010.

Gausa, Manuel. "In-between" and "Reversible". In *The Metapolis dictionary of advanced architecture: city, technology and society in the information age,* edited by Manuel Gausa, Vicente Guallart, Willy Muller, Federico Soriano, Fernando Porras, and Josè Morales, pp. 334, 528. Actar, 2003.

Gausa, Manuel. *Open. Espacio, tiempo, información.* Actar, 2010.

Girot, Christophe. "Vision in motion: representing landscape in time". In *The Landscape Urbanism Reader,* edited by Charles

Waldheim, pp. 87-103. Princeton Architectural Press, 2006.

Guallart, Vicente. (2013, July 17). City Protocol - Anatomy of City Habitat. YouTube. https:// www.youtube.com/watch?v=zs_ sNEfzvVY [accessed 20.02.2021].

Harvey, David. *Rebel cities. From the right to the city to the urban revolution.* Verso, 2012.

Hou, Jeffrey. "Guerrilla urbanism: urban design and the practices of resistance". *Urban Design International,* vol. 25 no. 2, 2020, pp. 117-125.

Jacobs, Jane. *Vita e morte delle grandi città.* Translated by Giuseppe Scattone. Edizioni di Comunità, 2000.

Lydon, Mike, and Anthony Garcia. *Tactical Urbanism: Short-term Action for Long-term Change.* Island Press, 2015.

Kennedy, Christopher, John Cuddihy, and Joshua Engel-Yan. "The changing metabolism of cities". *Journal of Industrial Ecology,* vol. 11, no. 2, 2007, pp.43-59.

Lefebvre, Henri. *Il diritto alla città.* Translated by Cesare Bairati. Marsilio, 1970.

Meroni, Anna. *Creative Communities: People inventing sustainable ways of living.* Polidesign, Milano, 2007.

Oswalt, Philipp, Klaus Overmeyer, and Philipp Misselwitz. *Urban catalyst: The power of temporary use.* Dom Publisher, 2013.

Ratti, Carlo. *Architettura open source.* Einaudi, 2014.

Ratti, Carlo. *La città di domani.* Einaudi, 2017.

Rauws,Ward Samue. *Why planning needs complexity: Towards*

an adaptive approach for guiding urban and peri-urban transformations. University of Groningen, 2015.

Rauws, Ward Samuel, and Gert De Roo. "Adaptive planning: Generating conditions for urban adaptability. Lessons from Dutch organic development strategies". *Environment and Planning B: Planning and Design,* vol. 43, no. 6, 2016, pp.1052–1074.

Ricci, Mosè. *Habitat 5.0. L'Architettura del Lungo Presente.* Skira, 2019.

Sennet, Richard. "The Open city". In *The Endless city,* edited by Ricky Burdett, and Deyan Sudjic, pp.290-297. Phaidon, 2007.

Sennet, Richard. *Costruire e abitare. Etica per la città.* Translated by Cristina Spinoglio. Feltrinelli, 2018.

Sennet, Richard. (2006, November). The Open City. Urbanage. https://urbanage.lsecities.net/ essays/the-open-city [accessed 12.01.2021].

Toffler, Alvin. *The Third Wave,* William Morrow and Company, 1980.

Wolman, Abel. "The Metabolism of Cities". *Scientific American,* no. 213, 1965 pp.179-90.

#Performative_tools

Urban challenges and resilient cities

Silvia Mannocci

Cities of the 21st century are facing profound social, economic, and environmental transformations that, unlike previous historical periods, occur extremely rapidly.

The structural changes of the last century, such as population growth, rapid urbanization, globalization, technological development and climate change have profoundly altered society, transforming it into what Zygmunt Bauman calls a "liquid society", characterized by more mobile, temporary and individualized living conditions. at the base of the complexities and problems of today's urban spaces, each of which contributes to a general state of uncertainty and crisis of the system, not least that caused by the pandemic emergency due to the spread of Covid-19, which has led to a further rapid change in our habits and the way we live the spaces of the city. It follows that it is not possible to think of the contemporary city as a defined spatial object to be read through a unitary point of view: the conventional concepts of place have been questioned by the spread of dense networks of physical and non-physical connections of which the city is composed, which return an image of the contemporary city that can be described as a set of processes, often disconnected from each other and constantly evolving and changing.

The issuance at international level of strategies and objectives that enshrine the need for urban development that can make cities more responsive to shocks and crises that may occur unexpectedly, has triggered in the debate on the territory the search for strategies to implement the adaptive capacity of the city so that they can be transformed into inclusive, safe, resilient, and sustainable environments (SDG 11).

In 2002, for the first time, the concept of ecological resilience was used in reference to the development of territorial systems in an official document of the European Union through the report "Resilience and Sustainable Development: Building Adaptive Capacity in a World of Transformations". The report was presented to the Swedish government's Environmental Advisory Council and was written by a group of scientists from the Resilience Alliance scientific network to share information on sustainable development with policymakers. The report supports the development of management strategies to improve ecosystem resilience and keep the three pillars of sustainability in balance: environment, society, and economy.

Resilience-building management is flexible and open to learning. It attends to slowly-changing, fundamental variables that create memory, legacy, diversity, and the capacity to innovate in both social and ecological components of the system. It also conserves and nurtures the diverse elements that are necessary to reorganize and adapt to novel, unexpected, and transformative circumstances. Thus, it increases the range of surprises with which a socio-economic system can cope (Folke et al. 2002).

At the heart of the paper drafted by the Resilience Alliance group of scientists is the approach to changes that can surprise socio-ecological systems. Change can be very slow and gradual or rapid and unexpected. Improving resilience means seizing the opportunity for transformation by taking a perspective of the system that is not frozen in time. From a resilient perspective, change is not strictly resisted, but is embraced through flexible management that is open to learning to innovate the social, environmental, and economic components of the internal system.

The sharing with policy makers of the report "Resilience and Sustainable Development: Building Adaptive Capacity in a World of Transformations" has triggered, in the international debate on land management, the search for strategies to make cities more responsive to shocks and crises that may occur unexpectedly. The document, in fact, was used as a basis for the implementation and updating of the contents of Agenda 21. In 2015, UN member states signed "The 2030 Agenda for Sustainable Development", a document that proposes 17 Sustainable Development Goals (SDGs), recognising that ending poverty and other deprivation requires going hand in hand with strategies that improve health and education, reduce inequalities and stimulate economic growth, all while tackling climate change and working to preserve the planet's natural resources. Goal 11 calls for making cities and human settlements inclusive, safe, resilient, and sustainable (SDG 2015).

In the contemporary debate on urban evolution, there is the possibility that theories and practices related to the concept of resilience are used as substitutes for theories and practices related to the concept of sustainability. The risk of making a purely linguistic substitution of the two terms is to trivialize both concepts without considering the potential that the use of the concept of resilience leads to the achievement of sustainability goals (Weller 2019).

In this research, resilience is treated as an extension of the concept of sustainability: a tool through which we can achieve sustainability goals and avoid potentially catastrophic regime changes (Pickett et al. 2013). The con-

01| SDGs integrated with Goal 11.

cept of resilience is closely related to the term crisis. The crisis is a powerful accelerator of the dynamics in place and often the sudden shock anticipates situations that would have occurred in the future due to the action of slow variables. But referring to the etymology of the word crisis, which comes from the Greek verb κρίνω - which means to separate, order, in a broader sense, discern, judge, evaluate - it is possible to recognize a positive connotation of the term. As often happens, the crisis can be an opportunity to criticize and reflect on the dynamics in place and to propose new solutions and alternative models of urban action. Right at the time of the crisis, the system should adopt a resilient perspective of sustainability: instead of aiming for balance by optimizing the performance of the system, the system should embrace change as an opportunity to create a new balance (Holling 2001).

As a theory and practice of negotiating change, resilience brings sustainability closer to the indeterminate way that both the natural and cultural worlds actually work. Whereas sustainability was based on an idealized ecology of equilibrium, resilience is based on an interpretation of nature as a constant state of disequilibrium. In theory disequilibrium is not the enemy of order; disequilibrium creates and propels life (Weller 2019).

The objective of achieving inclusive, safe, resilient, and sustainable cities required the evaluation of new types of governance of the local territory to exploit the co-benefits and complementarity offered by the interdependencies and interactions that exist within urban systems, with the aim of creating synergies aimed at sustainable development.

The 2030 Agenda for Sustainable Development states that the Sustainable Development Goals are integrated and indivisible and balance the three dimensions of sustainable development: economic, social and environmental (National Strategies and SDG Integration | Department of Economic and Social Affairs, no date).

In particular, Goal 11 is integrated with Goal 3: "Good Health and Well-being. Ensure a healthy life and promote well-being for all at all ages"; Goal 13: "Climate action. Take urgent action to combat climate change and its impacts." Goal 15: "Life on Earth. protect, restore and promote the sustainable use of terrestrial ecosystems, sustainably manage forests, combat desertification and halt and reverse land degradation and halt biodiversity loss"; Goal 16: "Peace, justice and strong institutions. Promote peaceful and inclusive societies for sustainable development, provide access to justice for all and build effective, accountable and inclusive institutions at all levels; Goal 17: "Partnership for goals. Strengthen the means of implementation and revitalize the global partnership for sustainable development" (SDGs 2015).

In this integrated and interconnected perspective, the concept of resilience becomes even more useful and central: it breaks down silos by providing a "conceptual umbrella" under which different disciplines come together to address complex problems with synergistic and holistic interventions.

Resilience

/riˈzilyəns/

Noun

1. the ability to become strong, healthy, or successful again after something bad happens
"The rescue workers showed remarkable resilience in dealing with the difficult conditions."

2. the ability of something to return to its original shape after it has been pulled, stretched, pressed, bent, etc.
"The resilience of rubber";
"Cold temperatures caused the material to lose resilience."

Etymology: The word resilience derives from the present participle of the Latin verb resilire, meaning "to jump back" or "to recoil." The base of resilire is salire, a verb meaning "to leap" that also pops up in the etymologies of such sprightly words as sally and somersault.

Merriam-Webster

The introduction in the vocabulary of urban planning and architecture of the term resilience, allows to assume a systemic point of view in the reading and management of urban dynamics able to include the traditional objectives of urban planning that aim to guarantee "an urban life that is at the same time beautiful, healthy, comfortable and economical" (Piccinato 1937) with the search for solutions to respond to the environmental crisis, in the ever-changing context of the contemporary city.

Through the concept of resilience and the ecological paradigm, we see the proposal of an interdisciplinary and interscalar approach to the hybridization of the territory, able to overcome the dualism of humanity and nature, with the aim of triggering the necessary ecological transition of the society of the XXI century, guided by the Oikeios concept, synthetic expression of oikeios topos, or "favorable place", a term coined by the Greek philosopher-botanist Theophrastus to indicate "the relationship between plant species and the environment" (Moore and Avallone 2015).

Resilience is a very broad concept, as is evident from the literary magazine on the subject. It is used in different disciplinary fields, with different meanings implying different visions and approaches to the concept of stability (Gunderson & Holling 2002). In this research, reference is made to the meaning of resilience used in ecology as a property of complex systems to react to stressful phenomena by adapting to change, not so much to return to their initial state, but aiming to restore functionality (Holling 1996).

Diversity, redundancy and variability are three indispensable characteristics of a resilient system, that is, a system capable of responding adaptively to change in order to be able to adapt quickly to new conditions even in the event of sudden crises and shocks (Holling 1973; Gunderson and Holling 2002; Walker and Salt 2012).

Resilience, in short, is largely about learning how to change in order not to be changed. Certainty is impossible. The point is to build systems that will be safe when they fail, not to try to build fail-safe systems. The goal of the resilient approach is to build systems that will be "safe-to-fail", not to try to build "fail-safe" systems (Ahern 2012).

This definition includes the system's ability to self-organize and adapt to change, concepts that make resilience more relevant to socio-ecological systems (Holling 1996, 2001; Levin et al. 1998; Carpenter et al. 2001; Folke 2006; Wu and Wu 2013).

It differs from the classic concept of equilibrium-centered resilience, called "engineering resilience," which focuses on efficiency, constancy, and predictability (Holling 1996).

"Ecological resilience theory suggests that what underlies a truly resilient city is not how stable it has appeared or how many little disturbances it has absorbed, but whether it can withstand an unforeseen shock that would fundamentally alter or erase the city's identity" (Wu and Wu 2013).

It is not intended to propose a new definition of urban resilience, but the concept is used as an extremely useful lens to analyze practices, projects and tools capable of acting simultaneously on several levels to ensure adaptive and multifunctional processes. In accordance with the holistic nature of the topic, a mosaic of projects, tools and strategies is proposed to improve the quality of urban life in 21st century cities.

This interpretative reading of projects and tools is organized according to five design characteristics (statements): Designing with the existing, Learning from the landscape, Co-designing with the community, Improving the network, Planning the unexpected. The structure of this investigation wants to retrace the changing nature of the investigated theme: connections and interferences articulate this path that combines different identities, different temporalities, and different modes of use.

Designing with the Existing

Designing with the Existing proposes a model of urban growth capable of reinhabiting and rehabilitating the existing building heritage, with the aim of avoiding the consumption of new land and promoting processes that support the circular economy in urban areas. The projects that fall into this category are those that do not follow the twentieth-century model of uncontrolled urban expansion, but that choose to work on the existing to adapt it, rather than replace it.

The approach called Designing with the Existing recognizes and emphasizes that the growth of the city does not correspond to its territorial extension or to the replacement tout court of obsolete structures, but supports a vision of urban growth that requires a dialogue between past and present, it is a matter of evolution and stratification rather than extension and cancellation.

Design with the existing is an approach that learns from the city and starts from the historical processes of urban evolution. Transformations are supported through deliberately "incomplete" projects (Sennett 2018) as in the case of the Social Housing project designed by Alejandro Aravena and Elemental in Iquique, Chile.

In contemporary architectural and urban language, the words "Regeneration", "Recycling", "Renaturalization" and "Recovery" have become part of the new territorial agendas rather recently, on the other hand they describe very well the way in which historically European cities and in particular Italian ones, have evolved, even if the urban planning regulations of the early twentieth century do not support them. Recycling and reusing existing buildings is an ancient and uninterrupted operation, as in the emblematic case of the Roman amphitheater of Arles transformed into a fortified citadel inhabited during the Middle Ages.

Using the words of architect Grasso Cannizzo, Designing with the existing considers architecture an open work (Marini and Cannizzo, 2014). The project is not the search for a completed set-up, but the definition of a moving device capable of transforming itself by assuming different shapes, roles and configurations. If necessary, the project overturns the codified rules and norms.

The project is only a possible answer in a precise time and not the definitive solution (Marini and Cannizzo, 2014).

02 | Before. Social Housing - Elemental, Iquique, Chile, 2003.Photo: © Cristobal Palma / Estudio Palmat

03| After. Social Housing - Elemental, Iquique, Chile, 2003. Photo: © Elemental

04 | Transformation of 530 housing units, Grand Parc district - Lacaton & Vassal, Druot, Hutin, Bordeaux, 2017. Photo: © Philippe Ruault

The resilient approach Designing with the Existing is an opportunity to reinterpret what we have already planned, prolongs the life expectancy of the built and proposes new innovative ways of intervention in the built urban context.

Learning from Landscape

Learning from Landscape proposes an approach to the city informed by landscape design processes to understand the operational dynamics of nature and enter synergy with it. According to J. Corner (2006), ecology represents a useful lens through which to analyze the fluid and non-linear developments of urban processes to design future urban developments in such a way that they are reactive and must anticipate change as well as respond to it:

In conceptualizing a more organic, fluid urbanism, ecology itself becomes an extremely useful lens through which to analyze and project alternative urban futures (Corner 2006, p.29).

Looking at the city with an ecological approach means considering cities a dynamic and complex system. In 1969, Ian L.

McHarg, with his text Design with Nature (1969), formalizes the indispensability of including ecological and environmental aspects within the planning and design processes. In Design with Nature man and nature, are not located in two distinct or opposing positions but "with", or together, in the same place.

The Alter Flugplatz project by Gnüchtel Triebswetter Landscape with Markus Gnuechtel, Roland Nagies and Klaus W. Rose in Frankfurt am Main is an example of a human-led project but implemented with the times of nature.

The former military heliport of Bonames was converted into a leisure park and nature reserve through a desealing action that allowed the pioneer species to colonize the area. The runways were fractured to restore greater permeability to the site and leave room for spontaneous plant colonization processes. The demolition material was partly reused in the park: the retaining walls were

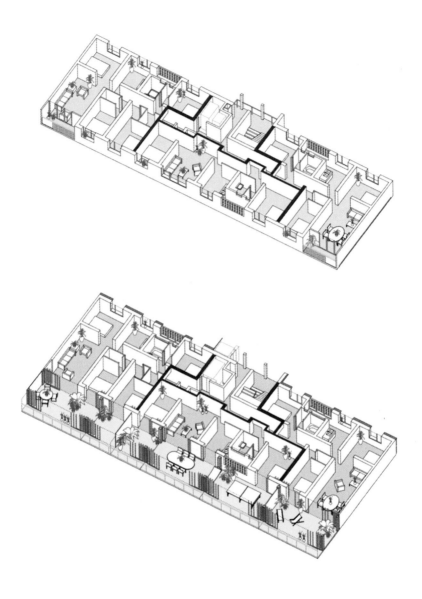

05 | Existing Axonometry_credit: © Lacaton & Vassal -Druot - Hutin

06 | Project axonometry_ credit: © Lacaton & Vassal - Druot - Hutin

made with metal gabions filled with demolition materials; or the concrete slabs of the helicopter landing pad make a rock garden. The main track has been completely preserved and reused as a route for sports. The ecological choice to limit demolitions and maximize the reuse of waste materials in situ has positive repercussions in economic terms also.

The resilient Learning from Landscape approach offers the opportunity to reinterpret what we have already planned, proposing new ways of intervening in the urban context in an ecological key. The designer learns from nature and the project becomes a trigger for a larger process that can evolve over time in an undeemly way.

Co-design with community

Co-design with community proposes actions able to awaken the sense of belonging of places through the active involvement of citizens, promoting the development of the territory through inclusive and co-creative urban planning. Resilient design requires local context knowledge and small-scale safe-to-fail approaches (Learning by doing). Safe-to-fail and Learning by doing allow you to proceed by trial and error and success. Fundamentally, the two approaches require a strong connection between knowledge and action and imply profound changes in our tradition of design, planning and management (Lister 2007). Diversity of skills, voices and professionalism are included in the design process to incentivize bottom-up responses to land management.

Co-design with community collects the design processes that improve social inclusion by increasing the sense of belonging and the skills of the local community. This type of initiative is based on the concept that to resist and react to the different and continuous changes in the urban context it is necessary to encourage the active action of citizens, to allow society to engage in processes of place-making and tactical urban planning to equip itself with the ability to respond in the event of a crisis.

Co-design with community collects projects that do not follow conventional and deterministic design processes, they are projects that realize forms and phenomena of radical resilience (Melis and Nava 2021).

These are phenomena of architectural exaptation: a functional "displacement" of a structure that already had a function or the functional co-optation of obsolete structures (Melis and Nava, 2021). For example, the phenomena of temporary appropriation of public space, which contribute to the resilience of neighborhoods, the health of communities and the increase in the life cycle of materials concern uses of space not foreseen in any conventional project (Melis and Nava, 2021). Strengthening Social Capital means increasing diversity, variability and redundancy of the actors and actions capable of influencing and

07 | Before, Runway at the old airport, 2008. @Nicolas17

08 | After, Runway at the old airport, 2008 @Nicolas17

transforming the territory. This stimulates creative and innovative processes, but also increases the level of complexity of the system that could generate conflicts.

The Co-design with Community approach also includes those projects capable of managing urban conflicts, creating a territory of confrontation in which interferences become an opportunity to identify new solutions.

Enhancing the Network

Enhancing the Network proposes design processes to amplify knowledge and improve the management of the metabolic flows of the city, both material and immaterial.

Knowing the urban metabolism does not only mean considering the strictly ecological processes (water cycle, energy, food production, waste and emissions) but it means thinking of the city as a place of progress, creativity and exchange (Russo 2015). In this sense, the city is perceived as a network of places, functions, uses, flows and actors, resources and non-linear multi-scale relationships, multi-scale relationships that change over time, even very quickly, intersecting and overlapping.

"The city is made up of environment, infrastructures, public space, nodes, information and citizens. A system of systems" (Guallart 2012).

In Urban Habitat by Vicente Guallart the city is a self-sufficient organism capable of using its available resources (physical and otherwise) and the exchange of information.

The redevelopment project of Tudela-Culip Club Med at the Parc Natural del Cap de Creus in Martì Franch (EMF) and his colleague Ton Ardèvol proposes an innovative approach to the theme of reuse by combining it with ecological rehabilitation and the circular economy. In 1960, a tourist village was built in Cap de Creus on the orinetal tip of the Iberian Peninsula. In 1998, Cap de Creus was declared a National Park and the promontory received the highest level of protection in the area due to its geological and botanical value. In the summer of 2003, the tourist village was closed and in 2005 the promontory was purchased by the Spanish Ministry of the Environment, which activated a recovery project. The project demolished the volumes of the tourist center, but in a circular economy, 45,000 cubic meters of demolition material were recycled and reused for the construction of the new paths to make the park usable.

The support of the technology is twofold: on the one hand it allows you to control the changes that are taking place in the system in real time; on the other hand, it allows you to exchange information more quickly. The Trash

09 | Superkilen, 2012. Urban park in Copenhagen. Red Square. Commissioned by City of Copenhagen and RealDania. BIG and Topotek1. Photo: ©Iwan Baan

10 | Superkilen, 2012. Urban park in Copenhagen. Green Park. Commissioned by City of Copenhagen and RealDania. Developed in close collaboration with Bjarke Ingels Group (BIG) and Topotek1.
Photo: ©Mike Magnussen

Track project of the Senseable City Lab of MIT in Boston obtains through the direct involvement of citizens a greater awareness of the issue of waste production and disposal. The project, through sensors positioned on the waste, traced the paths of the waste produced by a sample of 500 people, mapping where the product was disposed of. In this way, a broad awareness of the waste disposal process is acquired, making evident the connections that exist between waste management, space and related impacts.

Enhancing the Network resilient approach recognizes the metabolic functioning of the city. Enhancing the Network offers opportunities to enhance networks and relationships within the city. They are projects that create a point between the potential of technology and social capital for resource utilization through circular economy processes.

Planning the unexpected

Planning the unexpected addresses the issue of uncertainty arising from the dynamism of the contemporary urban environment, with particular attention to the search for solutions to adapt and mitigate the negative consequences of climate change. The needs of cities and citizens are constantly changing

12 | Above: Depave Paradise

– demography and business cycles, densification, new activities and new environmental conditions – and they need flexible spaces to accommodate these changing needs.

If a place is to be truly resilient, its urban form must be responsive and capable of change (Sim and Gehl 2019).

The urban projects that fall into this category are those that offer adaptive and multifunctional spaces to the city, spaces capable of reconfiguring themselves in case of extreme events, such as the Water Square designed by De

Urbanisten in Rotterdam. Water Squares perform a double function: they are both public space and areas of accumulation of excess rainwater. The square is part of the water system composed of canals and basins connected to each other, which have the task of collecting rainwater, mitigating the run-off phenomenon and reusing excess water to irrigate the surrounding greenery.

The variability of a space and its ability to evolve over time and adapt to new conditions also depends on the design approach that is assumed.

People use scenarios to envision alternative futures and the pathways by which they might be reached. By envisioning multiple alternative futures and actions that might attain or avoid particular outcomes, we can identify and choose resilience-building policies (Folke et al. 2002).

A project that can describe this kind of approach is proposed by James Corner Field Operation for the Tidal Basin in Washington, D.C. The Tindal Basin is a standout attraction along the National Mall, home to the Jefferson, FDR, and MLK memorials, as well as D.C's iconic cherry tree collection, whose flowers are celebrated every spring. Due to years of delayed maintenance and neglect, the tidal basin flood gates no longer function as originally intended, allowing the river to run past the gates at high tide. This, together

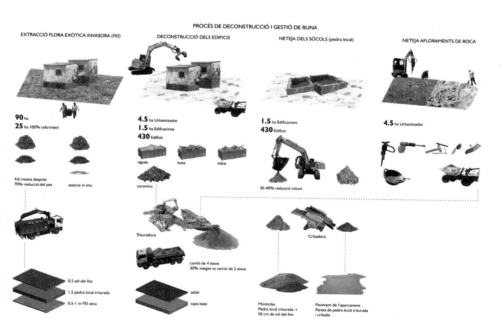

13 | Tudela-Culip Club Med. Demolition process and ruin management. Source: EMF

14 | Tudela-Culip Club Med. Before and after. Photo: ©Martì Franch
15 | Tudela-Culip Club Med. Totems. Photo: ©Pau Ardèvol

with the rise in the water level, due to climate change, in the Potomac, leads to the daily flooding of paths and cherry trees. Climate change is also producing increasingly intense and frequent storms, flooding the tidal basin, the National Mall and the surrounding urban fabric.

Field Operations proposes three scenarios, which together build an argument on the meaning of climate change problems and how to solve them. Each scenario considers a different approach: "Curate Entropy" embraces the inevitability of decline and decay through a naturalization process; "Island Archipelago" allows the waters of the Potomac to flood the tidal basin, and creates a new set of protective gardens around the monuments; and "Protect & Preserve" proposes a large ribbon of embankment with new walks along the river, completely protecting the tidal basin, monuments and cherry trees, creating more parks and opportunities for services and recreational activities. These future scenarios are neither objective nor neutral. The first two offer critiques of the trajectory of indecision and today's restrictive frameworks for conservation and restoration.

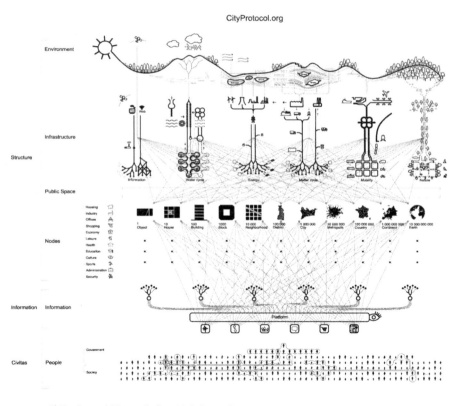

16 | City Protocol, Vicente Guallart, 2012, Source: Iaac.

The third postulates a scenario that is both reverent and far-sighted, designed and improvised, fixed and dynamic. In this sense, the project is not expressed only through notions of organization, rationalization but builds a vision capable of mobilizing subjects and resources to offer the city a hope for the future (Russo 2015)

Planning the Unexpected resilient approach takes change as an invariant of the urban environment and assimilates it within the projects and the design process. Planning the unexpected promotes design attitudes that reject determinism and offer multifunctional and flexible spaces that promote adaptive urban evolution.

Those projects, actions and tools that rehabilitate and re-inhabit the existing building are recognized as capable of implementing the resilience of the city, proposing a model of urban growth capable of responding to the growing demand for densification and opposing the consumption of new land; who do not seek to copy and imitate nature in its forms, but to understand the dynamics of its work to enter into synergy with it to overcome the dichotomy between man and nature; that exploit the potential offered by technological innovation to better know and manage the metabolic flows that cross the city; able to awaken the sense of belonging of places through the active involvement of citizens; and are able to respond to the contingent issues dictated by the negative consequences of climate change.

The aim is to underline the importance of triggering in the urban system a plurality of actions, able to act simultaneously on several levels to ensure processes adaptable to change and multifunctional.

Dealing with any single issue in isolation is not sufficient to address the resilience of the city as a whole. (Wu and Wu 2013).

Relationships, connections, and inferences link the five key concepts to each other.

Transdisciplinary and multi-scale articulate this process of multiple actions.

Each action works at different scales, by different timing, by different objectives and by the involvement of different actors.

The goal is to emphasize how it is necessary in a complex system like the city to propose the implementation of a plurality of practices that can ensure the activation at multiple levels of adaptable, self-organized and multifunctional processes. Planning for a resilient urban future requires tackling challenges and creating solutions in a place-based, integrated, inclusive, risk-aware, and forward-looking manner (Resilient cities Nerwork).

It is not a question of tracing a defined route but aims to return an open framework of possibilities in which are identified the various elements capable of triggering urban evolution.

17 | The water square Benthemplein the square in the rain. Photo: ©De Urbanisten

18 | The water square Benthemplein the square after the rain. Photo: ©De Urbanisten

19 | Aerial view of the BIG U's flood defence system. Source: BIG

Bibliographic references

Ahern, Jack. "From fail-safe to safe-to-fail: Sustainability and resilience in the new urban world". In *Landscape and Urban Planning*, 100, 2011. 341-343. 10.1016/j.landurbplan.2011.02.021.

Corner, James. "Terra fluxus". In *The landscape urbanism reader*, edited by Charles Waldheim, Architectural Press, 2006.

Folke, Carl, Steve Carpenter, Thomas Elmqvist, Lance Gunderson, C. S. Holling, Brian Walker. "Resilience and sustainable development: Building adaptive capacity in a world of transformations". In *Ambio*, 31(5), 2002, pp. 437–440. http://www.ncbi.nlm.nih.gov/ pubmed/12374053

Guallart, Vicente. *City Protocol - Anatomy of City Habitat*, video, 2012. https://www.youtube.com/watch?v=zs_sNEfzvVY [accessed 27.07.2018]

Gunderson, Lance H., and C.S. Holling. *Panarchy: understanding transformations in human and natural systems*, Island Press, Washington, DC, 2002.

Holling, Crawford Stanley "Engineering resilience versus ecological resilience". In *Engineering within ecological constraints*, edited by Peter Schulze, National Academy Press, Washington, DC, 1996.

Holling, Crawford Stanley "Understanding the complexity of economic, ecological, and social systems". In *Ecosystems*, 4, 2001, pp. 390–405.

Levin, Simon A. "Ecosystems and the biosphere as complex adaptive systems". In *Ecosystems*, 1, 1998, pp. 431–436.

Lister, Nina-Marie. "Sustainable Large Parks: ecological design or designer ecology?" In *Large parks*, edited by Julia Czerniak and George Hargreaves, Princeton Architectural Press, New York, 2007, pp. 35-57.

Marini, Sara, and Maria Giuseppina Grasso Cannizzo. *Loose ends: Maria Giuseppina Grasso Cannizzo*. S.l: Aut. Architektur und Tirol, 2014.

McHarg, Ian L. *Design with nature*. Wiley-Blackwell, Garden City, NJ, USA, 1969.

Melis, Alessandro, and Consuelo Nava. "Un paradigma radicale bioecologico per le tecnologie progettanti con approccio transdisciplinare". In *Techne*, 21, Firenze University Press, 2021, pp. 103-111DOI: 10.36253/techne-9938

Moore, Jason W. *Ecologia-mondo e crisi del capitalismo: la fine della natura a buon mercato*. Ombre corte, Verona, 2015.

Piccinato, Luigi. "URBANISTICA". In *Enciclopedia Italiana* [online] (n.d.). Treccani, il portale del sapere, 1937 [accessed 11.01.2018]. https://www.treccani.it/enciclopedia/urbanistica_res-2bd3b412-8bb8-11dc-8e9d-0016357eee51 (Enciclopedia-Italiana)/

Pickett, Steward T.A., Mary Cadenasso, and Brian McGrath. *Resilience in ecology and urban design: linking theory and practice for sustainable cities*. Springer, 2013.

Russo, Michelangelo. "Un nuovo orizzonte temporale per il progetto urbanistico". In *Urbanistica*, 2015.

Sennett, Richard. *Costruire e abitare: etica per la città*. Feltrinelli, Milano, 2018.

Sim, David, and Jan Gehl. *Soft city: building density for everyday life*. Island Press, Washington, District of Columbia, 2019.

Walker, Brian, and David Salt. *Resilience Practice: Building Capacity to Absorb Disturbance and Maintain Function*. Springer Nature, 2012. 10.5822/978-1-61091-231-0.

Weller, Richard. "Sostenibilità resiliente". In *Architettura del Paesaggio*. Changes, 38, 2019, pp. 10-13. https://static1.squarespace.com/static/56b5181b2eeb812c644 99929/t/5d388caf3440e70 00153 1d77/1563987119722/resilient+sustainability+pdf.pdf

Wu, Jianguo, and Tong Wu. "Ecological resilience as a foundation for urban design and sustainability". In *Resilience in Urban Ecology and Design: Linking Theory and Practice for Sustainable Cities*, edited by Steward T.A. Pickett, Mary L. Cadenasso, and Brian P. McGrath, Springer, 2013.

Sitography

BIG | Bjarke Ingels Group, https://big.dk/#projects [accessed 03.03.2018].

Büro / Team - GTL-Michael Triebswetter, https://gtl-landschaftsarchitektur.de/buero-profil/ [accessed 18.07.2019].

Comunità Resilienti | Padiglione Italia Biennale Architettura 2021 https://www.comunitaresilienti.com/ [accessed 15.6.2021].

DE URBANISTEN https://www.urbanisten.nl/ [accessed 09.01.2018].

Depave | From Parking Lots to Paradise, https://depave.org/ [accessed 02.02.2018].

EMF | Estudi Martí Franch | Arquitectura del Paisatge, http://www.emf.cat/ [accessed 03.01.2018].

Field Operations - home, https://www.fieldoperations.net/home.html [accessed 16.04.2021].

Freshkills Park, https://freshkillspark.org/ [accessed 18.05.2018].

ICLEI. *Thriving Cities: The Evolution Of Urban Resilience*, https://www.iclei.org/en/publication/resilient-cities-thriving-cities-the-evolution-of-urban-resilience#:~:text=This%20report%20uses%20the%20decade,next%20decade%20of%20bold%20action [accessed 13.03.2021].

Lacaton & Vassal, https://www.lacatonvassal.com/ [accessed 15.04.2019].

Melis, Alessandro. *Resilienza radicale*. Presentation at the 25° Fondazione dell'Ordine degli Architetti di Lecco "La pluralità della bellezza", Lecco. https://www.youtube.com/watch?v=-9j8KE4N9fQA [accessed 08.11.2019]

Merriam-Webster. *Resilience*. In Merriam-Webster'.com dictionary. https://www.merriam-webster.com/dictionary/resilience [accessed 20.11.2017].

National strategies and SDG integration | Department of Economic and Social Affairs — Sustainable Development, https://sdgs.un.org/topics/national-sustainable-development-strategies [accessed 04.02.2019].

Resilient Cities Network —Urban Resilience, https://resilientcitiesnetwork.org/urban-resilience/ [accessed 22.10.2021].

Superkilen – Superflex, https://superflex.net/works/superkilen [accessed 03.03.2018].

Superkilen — Topotek 1, https://www.topotek1.de/openSpaces/superkilen-2/ [accessed 27.02.2019].

Topotek 1, https://www.topotek1.de/ [accessed 03.03.2018].

Turenscape, https://www.turenscape.com [accessed 03.05.2018].

Urban Resilience Hub, http://urbanresiliencehub.org/what-is-urban-resilience/ [accessed 12.03.2018].

46°05'25.0"N 11°05'50.7"E

Trento No 1

#Performative_tools

Climate sensitive urban regeneration

Anna Codemo

Framework

Urbanization and growth of urban population have been increasing at an unprecedented rate, leading to a variety of political, economic, climatic, ecological challenges. Particularly, loss of biodiversity, climate change and soil consumption have been questioning the role of cities for a transition towards healthier and more liveable human habitats. The built environment is the major contributor to climate change, due to the levels of energy consumption and greenhouse emissions. Moreover, it is vulnerable to the effects of climate change, causing risks for infrastructures, services and people (JPI 2019). However, cities represent a field of intervention and an opportunity for the transition towards a cleaner future. Being cities hubs of networks, the United Nations (UN) and European Commission (EC) targeted them in one of the 17 Sustainable Development Goals (SDGs) in the 2030 Agenda for Sustainable Development (UN 2015), and in the Pact of Amsterdam, defining the European Urban Agenda.

To advance the envisioned transition, both climate adaptation and mitigation strategies need to be undertaken for the urban metabolism and the regeneration of the built environment. A good balance between mitigation and adaptation actions should be promoted, to simultaneously reduce emissions and create a robust and healthier environment (JPI 2019). Cities offer unique opportunities for changes, since most of the actions to mitigate and adapt to climate change are taken at the city level through planning, land use policies, energy, waste and transport regulations. However, the implementation of climate-related strategies is obstacled by the lack of adaptive and novel planning tools, and by the scarce capacity to coordinate multiple scales and sectors at the local level (Magni et al. 2021). Another barrier consists of the transformation of the existing heritage (Giorgi et al. 2020), which needs to be part of this transition through regeneration and reuse rather than demolition.

In this framework, the built environment needs to be transformed according to a regenerative approach, shifting from the "less bad" to the "more good" thinking. In other words, the targets need to shift from the neutral energy use to the positive energy, from the reduction of the environmental impacts to the provision of positive benefits, from mitigating the impacts to reversing the causes.

In this context, a holistic approach including climate, water, and waste is needed to achieve healthy and resilient urban areas. Regenerative design is based on three main pillars: climate and energy, carbon and ecology, and human wellbeing. Considering the synergic relationship between human, ecosystems and climate health, urban transformation in cities can be a regenerative resource to adapt and harmonize with climatic flows, to balance the use and production of energy, to provide positive environmental benefits, and focusing on salutogenic health and social justice. Hence, the built environment should be designed with climate (Olgyay 2015), with nature (McHarg 1969) and with people (Antonovsky 1979).

This study focuses on the energy and climate transition and aims to propose an integrated climate sensitive approach towards low energy, adaptive and healthy interventions, by guiding the transformation of the existing built environment, considering multiple purposes and scales of intervention. It investigates the physical characteristics of the built environment influencing the climate related challenges and their interrelations, and it defines an analytical framework for design practices to prioritize solutions achieving multiple functions. The proposed solutions include the combination of Nature-based (NbS), Renewable Energy Sources (RES)-based and energy efficient technologies solutions for open spaces and buildings.

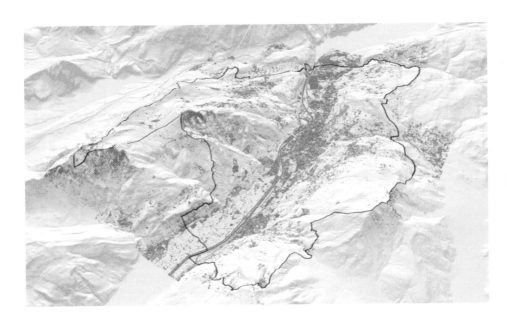

01 | Spatial distribution of the impervious surfaces of the Municipality of Trento.

Climate-related challenges in the urban environment

We must adapt to a world in which the climate is less predictable and less favorable, by scaling up mitigation and adaptation measures. To address climate change, urban transformations should integrate mitigation strategies - reducing greenhouse emissions -, with adaptation ones - to prepare for the effects of climate change. In line with the framework of the Trento Urban Transformations research project the present study sets four climate-related challenges, based on the European Agenda, to be achieved through small actions, allowing flexibility and continuous development of strategies and tactics. They are: temperature regulation, sustainable water management, inhabitant's health and wellbeing and energy sustainability. Each challenge is further defined by specific objectives and can be tackled by specific performances of the built environment. The specific objectives represent actions that can be implemented by urban transformations, and define the goals of a specific action; while, the performances constitute the drivers to implement the specific objectives, indicating possible tools and quantitative criteria used by practitioners. The definition of the performances relies on the relationship between the built environment and the urban climate, and depends on the parameters of their interactions. Such a methodological framework is flexible and can be modified according to the site condition.

Temperature regulation

Temperature regulation is the challenge related to urban climate and microclimate. Densification and land take of the urban environment, led to the phenomenon of Urban Heat Island (UHI), consisting of higher temperatures in the urban areas compared to the surrounding rural ones. Its main causes rely on morphological and physical characteristics of the built environment, as well as anthropogenic factors such as traffic and cooling systems. Moreover, UHI is exacerbated by global warming and heat waves, being a risk for health and comfort of people (Stewart & Oke 2012).

Sustainable Water Management

Integrated water quality and quantity management are important issues of urbanization. The uncontrolled growth of soil sealing and of urban population have been challenging stormwater management and water demand. The traditional management of water, based on directing runoff to waterways through the sewer system, is no longer able to respond to such phenomena. A

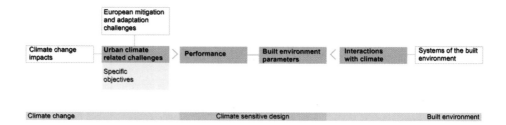

02 | Methodological approach to define performances and parameters of the built environment to tackle the climate-related challenges.

shift is foreseen towards a diffuse rainwater management, considering water as a resource and based on a localized and diffuse lamination, natural depuration, water reuse and infiltration in the soil. Sustainable water management can be achieved by land use transformation and the use of vegetation and pervious surfaces capable of infiltrating, retaining and purifying runoff (Charlesworth and Booth 2016).

Energy sustainability

The regeneration of the existing heritage is a key action to limit greenhouse emissions and to contribute to climate change mitigation. In line with the European policies, mitigation can be addressed by producing local energy from RESs, retrofitting the built environment to improve energy performances, and reducing emissions by energy saving (EC 2018). To optimally guarantee the energy demand, the interactions of the surroundings with the urban environment and buildings should be taken into account.

Health and wellbeing

Urban regeneration aims to improve social quality of life, livability and health, by making urban spaces more attractive (Marselle et al. 2019). Design practices, at any scale, should promote health of individuals, communities and ecosystems, enabling collaboration, participation, and open knowledge exchange, and transform the impact of cities by connecting to the place and to the people (Wahl 2016).

Urban climate and built environment: interactions and performances

Historically, the emphasis has been on managing conflicts between people and ecosystems, between people and climate. Now, there is a need to look at how these systems can work together, recognizing that healthy societies rely on healthy ecosystems. The climate-related challenges, including specific objectives and performances, involve actions at various scales of interventions, through different disciplines, in both public and private properties. With a multiscalar perspective, every action implemented can be part of a broader vision contributing to the climate challenges and improving the quality of the site and its microclimate, especially if the result is a connected network of urban spaces. To make decisions, it is necessary to use evidence coming from domain specific models, which may have different scales and relate to various disciplines. This may seem a difficult barrier to overcome, especially for small scale projects. However, domain-specific models' input parameters are phy-

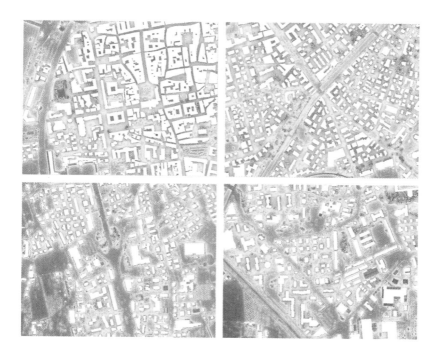

03 | Urban geometry: map of Sky View Factor in different districts of Trento, Italy

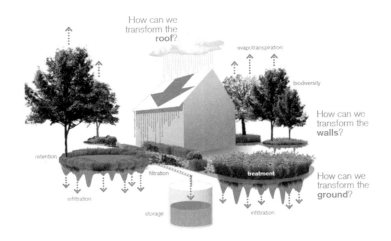

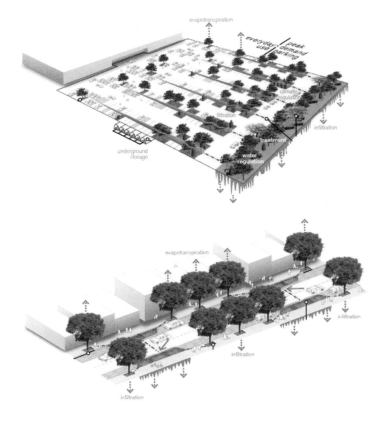

04| Use of Sustainable Urban Drainage Systems at different implementation scales. Source: UACDC, 2010

sical variables, which often are common to different disciplines. Therefore, the comprehension of the relationship between urban climate and built environment in relation to the different challenges, by defining mechanisms and parameters involved, facilitates the implementation of an integrated climate sensitive approach. To effectively express such interactions, the built environment can be categorized in four systems: urban geometry, vegetation, water bodies and surfaces (Lai et al. 2019).

To sum up this complex network of interactions, a simplification of the interactions is outlined, highlighting the implications on the climate challenges and the interactions of the parameters. Regarding the challenge of temperature regulation, the physical parameters used to describe the thermal environment are air temperature, thermal radiation, wind speed and humidity. They are independent from each other, but they can be integrated to calculate equivalent temperature, which is a parameter used to evaluate outdoor thermal comfort. Based on the studies reviewed, the characteristics of the built environment interacting with climate, which can drive the choice of the design solutions, are ventilation, shading, albedo, greening, evapotranspiration, soil filtration, water storage and emissions reduction. Particularly, temperature regulation can be tackled by intervening on ventilation, shading, albedo, use of greening and evapotranspiration. Changing such characteristics can reduce surface and air temperature, improve outdoor thermal comfort and block solar radiation, thus reducing the UHI effect and improving local microclimate.

The enabling processes related to sustainable water management used to describe the behavior of water entering the urban systems as precipitation are conveyance, infiltration, detention, retention, evapotranspiration, and treatment. The parameters influencing these processes are permeability, water storage capacity and greening. For example, by using pervious surfaces, it is possible to reestablish more natural water balances, to reduce runoff peaks and volumes and promote infiltration, retention and evapotranspiration. By integrating urban greening, it is possible to contribute to groundwater recharge through infiltration processes, and land restoration can increase the water holding capacity of natural land upstream of urban areas. Sustainable water management can be achieved by the use of greenery, water storage and soil filtration, which allow temporary water retention, storage and reuse of rainwater and improvement of water quality.

Energy sustainability can be pursued by working on emission reduction, use of green and indirectly on ventilation, shading, evapotranspiration and albedo, since they reduce the need to use cooling systems. Health and well-being of the inhabitants can be obtained with actions on greening and on shading, which contribute to create green and social areas as well as to improve air quality.

05 | Green infrastructure: map of urban greening of the Municipality of Trento, Italy

The parameters of the built environment interacting with urban climate have been collected and combined with the parameters influencing sustainable water management, energy consumptions and health and wellbeing. Such parameters become drivers for urban transformations through a climate sensitive design approach. An overall picture of these characteristics emerges illustrating the multiple interactions between them and supporting the definition of a holistic approach and tools for design and planning practices.

The effectiveness of solutions on the climate-related challenges is different and depends on several factors, such as the location, the type of soil, and urban compactness. For this reason, the choice of the specific solutions depends on the area of study.

Towards an integrated approach based on systems

A net-positive and holistic approach constitutes a change of paradigm from the mono-disciplinary perspective, as promoted by the SDGs and the Urban Challenges of JPI (SRIA). In this view, urban transformations become catalysts of change aiming to enhance the relationship between natural systems, built environment and inhabitants. Focusing on the climate and energy challenges, regenerative design requires an understanding of local dynamics, of interactions with climate and microclimate and with ecosystems. This approach entails a network of several disciplines, such as climate, ecology, human health and demands an interdisciplinary system thinking by designers and decision-makers. The awareness of the need to combine positive energy requirements with environmental criteria pushed for parametric design methods at the neighbourhood level to facilitate optimization, substituting traditional methods such as Multi-Criteria Decision Analysis based on weighting systems.

An integrated approach to urban regeneration is a multi-domain system which needs to be approached from multidisciplinary experts framing common goals, which will guide the development of scenarios. This approach facilitates the process of negotiation of acceptable ranges for common design parameters rather than weighting key performance indicators at the end of the process.

A system-based design approach is envisioned to guide the transformation of the urban environment to achieve multiple benefits, defined by some key ideas. The first one acknowledges the built environment as a local system. In other words, the characterization of the area: investigating the environmental characteristics (i.e. understanding the current situation of climate-related performances), defining the urban geometry (i.e. assessment of urban systems: blue and green infrastructure, morphology and surfaces) and the urban quality to identify systems or spaces that require regeneration.

200m   400m   600m

200m

200m

400m

600m

▓▓ Green Infrastrastructure
▓░ Blue Infrastrastructure (open, covered)
▓ ▓ Land surface temperature, from Landsat OLI

06 | Blue and Green Infrastructure and Land Surface Temperature in a commercial and residential district in the North of Trento, Italy

The results are used to identify the performances that need to be improved in the area, aiming to regenerate the urban environment to be prepared for future scenarios, to be neutral in terms of emissions and to foster quality and safety in the space. To address such challenges, the proposed framework insists on three main concepts.

Preparedness. The capacity of the built environment to address the impacts of climate change, for example those related to urban heat island and extreme heat events as well as extreme rain events.

Positive. Transformations of the urban areas should be energy efficient and reduce carbon emissions, while producing energy locally from RESs.

Care. The built environment can contribute to improve comfort and quality of life for the inhabitants.

Considering the four afore-mentioned concepts to transform the built environment, seven possible systems of intervention have been outlined, characterized by different levels of complexity and scales: (1) morphology of built

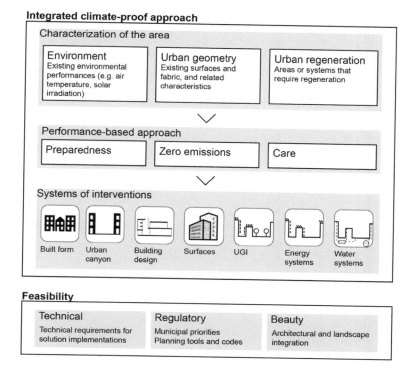

07 | Methodological framework to guide integrate climate proof regeneration

form, by addition or removal of volumes, (2) urban canyon, by changing the ratio between buildings and open spaces, (3) building design, by promoting bioclimatic and passive solutions at the design stage, (4) surfaces of the envelopes as well as of the open spaces, (5) Blue and Green Infrastructure, which should be enhanced considering the multiple functions, (6) energy systems, to improve energy efficiency as well as energy production from renewable sources, (7) water systems, to store and reuse water.

The role of surfaces in regeneration processes

The challenge is to get inspiration from the best practices and make them the standard. To achieve this we need to transform the existing heritage, by reconsidering the interactions between the built environment and the climate. The baseline concept for an integrated approach is to not consider the buildings and open spaces as individual objects but as part of a system, in which the envelopes are a diaphragm between outdoor and indoor environment. To transform the existing heritage through a regenerative approach, it is crucial to acknowledge the systems and consider them in the design process. With such a shift, the interactions between the built environment and humans, and climate-related benefits may be achieved. As the aim of the study is the transformation of the existing built environment, the focus of the solutions is the transformation of the surfaces, rather than the morphology. According to recent studies, surfaces have a key role to tackle several challenges in the urban environment due to their properties.

By urban surfaces, we can consider buildings' envelopes as well as ground areas. The latter include linear elements, such as streets, and open spaces, such as parking lots. The former is divided into roofs, facades and additional tridimensional elements. An extensive literature investigation has been done to collect solutions to transform surfaces to tackle the climate-related challenges. These have been categorized in: Urban Green Infrastructure, Blue Infrastructure, Energy Systems, Shading devices, Building technologies. Each category is further divided in sub-categories, according to the type of solution.

Urban Green Infrastructure

UGI provides many ecosystem services (e.g. balancing water flows, providing thermal comfort), contributing to ecosystem resilience and bio-physical, social, psychological benefits (Demuzere et al. 2014). It is an infrastructure of built systems and green spaces, including large-scale elements such as wetlands, forests, parks, and small-scale elements such as green roofs and green facades.

Urban regeneration

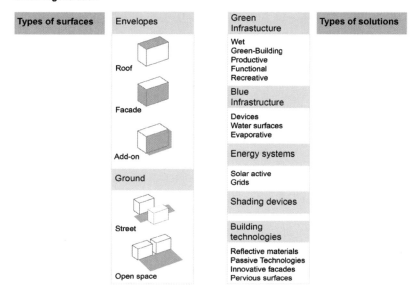

Types of surfaces	Envelopes	Green Infrastructure	Types of solutions

Roof

Facade

Add-on

Ground

Street

Open space

Green Infrastructure

Wet
Green-Building
Productive
Functional
Recreative

Blue Infrastructure

Devices
Water surfaces
Evaporative

Energy systems

Solar active
Grids

Shading devices

Building technologies

Reflective materials
Passive Technologies
Innovative facades
Pervious surfaces

08 | Types of surfaces available for climate sensitive regeneration and categorization of solutions.

Blue Infrastructure

BI provides benefits in sustainable water management as well as in cooling, through evaporation. It includes: natural water surfaces, such as rivers and lakes; artificial ones, such as canals; techniques like spaying and water curtains, which can be applied to ground surfaces as well as to buildings (Santamouris et al. 2017).

Energy systems

ES include systems in urban areas that can generate energy locally produced from RES, to meet energy requirements (heating, cooling, electricity, hot water). Clean energy in built-up areas is mostly produced by active solar systems, applied in buildings' surfaces or on-ground, as well as by grid systems that connect multiple buildings.

Shading devices

S include solutions to protect from direct solar radiation, to adapt to the increase of temperature and to reduce the buildings' energy needs. Shading devices solutions can be applied to buildings surfaces, as well as to open spaces.

Building Technologies

BT refer to the adaptive technologies, which rely on passive design to improve building energy efficiency and, indirectly, outdoor thermal regulation. These solutions include the techniques applied to buildings' envelopes to encourage natural ventilation and maximize direct solar gains.

Rethinking building skins

Building envelopes constitute a diaphragm between the indoor and outdoor environment, and represent an opportunity to combine the energy challenges of the built environment, with the environmental performances related to climate adaptation. In regeneration processes, envelopes can be retrofitted by using passive technologies, and active technologies locally producing energy from renewable energy sources.

9 | Retrofitting of the office building MA 31 in Vienna with a green facade. Source: Gruenstattgrau

Some of the functions embraced by buildings skins related to the climate challenges are:

- Facilitating natural ventilation to reduce energy consumptions for air conditioning (e.g. through double skin facades);
- Increasing direct solar gain to reduce energy consumptions for heating (e.g. through solar greenhouse, regenerative PCM-facades, double skins facades);
- Controlling heat transmission to reduce energy losses (e.g. through insulation and green roofs);
- Increasing solar reflectance to reduce energy consumptions for air conditioning (e.g. through cool roofs and cool facades);
- Locally producing energy from RES (e.g. through photovoltaic panels and thermal solar);
- Collecting and reusing rainwater to reduce runoff (e.g. with using green and wet roofs).

Integrating nature in open spaces

Nature-based solutions are inspired and supported by nature and use natural processes to address societal challenges. Moreover, they contribute to several

10 | Blankenstraat in Amsterdam: car-free area and integration of NbS. Source: Climatescan

economic, social, environmental benefits. Nature's interaction with the physical space occur at every scale, from the interior of a building to regions. Specifically, nature can be brought to urban surfaces such as streets and open spaces to contribute to the societal challenges. The integration of nature in open spaces contributes to several benefits: improving health and wellbeing of people, creating more comfortable outdoor areas, managing urban water in a sustainable way, as well as indirectly reducing buildings' energy consumption.

The climate-related functions of the open spaces integrated with UGI and BI are as follows (e.g. Akbari et al. 2012):

— Facilitating ventilation, to reduce air temperature;
— Increasing evapotranspiration, to reduce surface and air temperature as well as to manage rainwater;
— Improving soil infiltration to temporarily retain water and reduce runoff;
— Maintaining groundwater levels, preventing low river flows in summer and reducing the amount of wastewater.

Moreover, the use of Sustainable Urban Drainage Systems (SUDS) improves water quality, by reducing the amount of contaminants, enhances biodiversity and provides valuable habitats and urban quality features.

Regenerative design for cities

The regenerative approach in design and planning practices aims to go beyond sustainable development and to proactively contribute to reinforce urban ecosystems. The new tasks for decision-makers and practitioners consist in the creation of pleasant and healthy areas as well as in guaranteeing their resilience. The creation of secure, pleasant, recreational human habitats gives the opportunity to environmentally and ecologically restore cities.

Local context, built environment systems and performances become three key elements to integrate regenerative design principles in design and planning practices and interrelating humans, built environment and natural systems.

Bibliographic references

Akbari, Hashem, and H. Damon Matthews. "Global Cooling Updates: Reflective Roofs and Pavements." *Energy and Buildings* 55, 2012, pp. 2–6. https://doi.org/10.1016/j.enbuild.2012.02.055.

Antonovsky, Aaron. *Health, Stress, and Coping.* Edited by Jossey-Bass. San Francisco, 1979.

Charlesworth, Susanne M., and Colin A. Booth. *Sustainable Surface Water Management: A Handbook for SUDS.* John Wiley & Sons, 2016.

Demuzere, Matthias, Kati Orru, Oliver Heidrich, Eduardo Olazabal, Davide Geneletti, Hans Orru, Ajay Gajanan Bhave, Neha Mittal, Efrén Feliu, and Maija Faehnle. "Mitigating and Adapting to Climate Change: Multi-Functional and Multi-Scale Assessment of Green Urban Infrastructure." In *Journal of Environmental Management* 146 (December), 2014, pp. 107–15. https://doi.org/10.1016/j.jenvman.2014.07.025.

European Commission. 2018. "A Clean Planet for All. A European Long-Term Strategic Vision for a Prosperous, Modern, Competitive and Climate Neutral Economy." Com(2018) 773, 25. https://eur-lex.europa.eu/legal-content/EN/TXT/PDF/?uri=CELEX-:52018DC0773&from=EN.

Giorgi, Serena, Monica Lavagna, and Andrea Campioli. "Circular Economy and Regeneration of Building Stock: Policy Improvements, Stakeholder Networking and Life Cycle Tools." In *Regeneration of the Built Environment from a Circular Economy Perspective*, edited by Stefano della Torre, Sara Cattaneo, Camilla Lenzi, and Alessandra Zanelli, 2020, pp. 291–301. Cham: Springer International Publishing. https://doi.org/10.1007/978-3-030-33256-3_27.

Joint Programming Initiative Urban Europe. "Strategic Research and Innovation Agenda 2.0", 2019. https://jpi-urbaneurope.eu/app/uploads/2019/02/SRIA2.0.pdf.

Lai, Dayi, Wenyu Liu, Tingting Gan, Kuixing Liu, and Qingyan Chen. "A Review of Mitigating Strategies to Improve the Thermal Environment and Thermal Comfort in Urban Outdoor Spaces." *Science of the Total Environment* 661, 2019, pp. 337–53.

Magni, Filippo, Giovanni Litt, and Giovanni Carraretto. 2021. "Metropolitan Cities Supporting Local Adaptation Processes. The Case of the Metropolitan City of Venice." *TeMA - Journal of Land Use, Mobility and Environment* 14 (2): 125–44. www.tema.unina.it.

Marselle, Melissa R., Jutta Stadler, Horst Korn, Katherine N. Irvine, and Aletta Bonn. "Biodiversity and Health in the Face of Climate Change: Challenges, Opportunities and Evidence Gaps." In *Biodiversity and Health in the Face of Climate Change*, edited by Melissa R. Marselle, Jutta Stadler, Horst Korn, Katherine N. Irvine, and Aletta Bonn, 2019, pp. 1–13. Cham: Springer International Publishing. https://doi.org/10.1007/978-3-030-02318-8_1.

McHarg, Ian L. *Design with Nature.* Edited by University of Pennsylvania. New York, 1969.

Olgyay, Victor. *Design with Climate: Bioclimatic Approach to Architectural Regionalism.* Edited by Princeton university press. Princeton and Oxford, 2015.

Santamouris, Mat. "Using Cool Pavements as a Mitigation Strategy to Fight Urban Heat Island—A Review of the Actual Developments." In *Renewable and Sustainable Energy Reviews* 26, 2013, pp. 224–40.

Stewart, Iain, and Timothy R. Oke. "Local Climate Zones for Urban Temperature Studies". In *Bulletin of the American Meteorological Society* 93, 2012, pp. 1879–1900.

United Nations. Durban Platform for Enhanced Action (decision 1/CP.17). *Adoption of a protocol, another legal instrument, or an agreed outcome with legal force under the Convention applicable to all Parties.* Adoption of the Paris Agreement. UNFCCC Paris, 2015.

University of Arkansas Community Design Center UACDC. 2010. *LID Low Impact Development. A design manual for urban areas.* University of Arkansas Press. Fayetteville.

Wahl, Daniel C. 2016. *Designing Regenerative Cultures.* Triarchy Press. International Futures Forum.

#Performative_tools

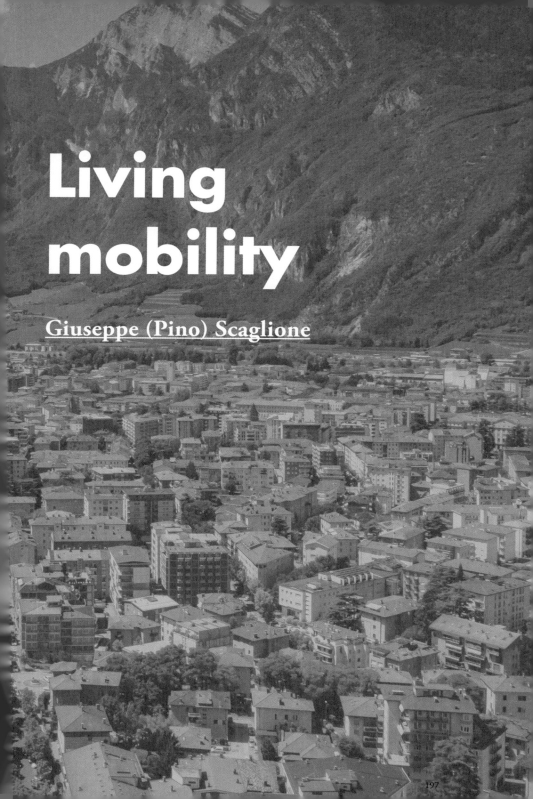

Living mobility

Giuseppe (Pino) Scaglione

Preface

Described by Paul Rudolph as the 'brick of the 20th century', the *mobile home* can be considered both a vehicle, in the moment of transport from the factory to the place of use, and home in the moment of use. Rudoplh wrote in 1950, that "... The fast-moving vehicle has transformed the possibilities of scale as an architectural tool to help us remember our humanity. Our transport modes will change in unpredictable ways, but the population explosion assures us that 'get there/reach/connect' will be a constant theme, and this will change our understanding of the environment" (Drexler and Rudolph 1970).

Updating Rudolph's thesis, Andrea Branzi recently wrote that, "in our commercial civilisation, the concept of an immobile urban fabric, rooted on its own foundations, marked by a definitive road network, is giving way to a different logic, more akin to the commodity philosophy of the market, where products are by their very nature transferable, removable, purchasable, decontextualisable. This leads to the hypothesis of a *city with variable boundaries*. We can say that our cities, apparently rigid and specialised, are actually mobile within themselves. So that the theme of a *mobile urban architecture* resurfaces today as a symptom of the fragility in our social foundations, dispersed by computer systems and the crisis of all ideologies" (Branzi 2018)

Yona Friedman, during the 1950s, developed a new architectural concept - in collaboration with the GEAM group *'Groupe d'étude d'architecture mobile'*. Friedman, in 1958, published a manifesto called 'Architecture Mobile' aimed at promoting a new type of citizen who was free and able to conquer space through large 'superstructures' on existing cities.

The Israeli-Hungarian architect's idea started from his perception that the increase of leisure time would profoundly change society, so cities would have to adapt to the new era. Another element of this *'Architecture Mobile'* idea was the possibility of periodically reshaping the individual habitat and urban layout, without imposing demolitions (Friedman 1960; Friedman, Frampton and Rodríguez 2011).

In practice, Friedman does no more than take up and take to extremes the extraordinary suggestions and research that Antonio Sant'Elia and the Futurists had already initiated in the 1920s, and later Le Corbusier with the Ville Radieuse or Frank Lloyd Wright with Broadacre City, the Dutch Constant, the English Archigram, up to the Italians Archizoom and Superstudio, and Branzi himself, who drew continuous and original ideas and reflections from these experiences.

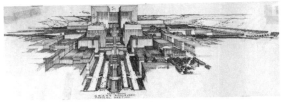

01 | Future city, Antonio Sant'Elia (1914)

02 03 | Two drawings by Hugh Ferriss investigating the real issues of Manhattanism, in "and Metropolis of Tomorrow, a 1929 book, Ferries includes drawings of existing skyscrapers, trends, and the future of the city. Undisputed protagonists are the means of transport. Source: http://www.frontiere.eu/antonio-santelia-centanni-dallamorte-

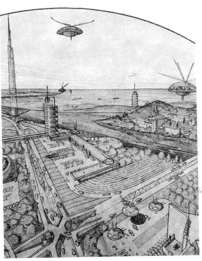

04 | Walkable New York with underground car traffic; Wiley Corbett (1928). Source: http://www.frontiere.eu/antonio-santelia-centanni-dallamorte-parte-terza-architettura-futurismo/

05 | Frank Lloyd Wright, drawing by Broadacre city, (1928)..

This branch of study and research also gave rise to the undoubtedly most ecologically advanced Italian experience, due to the intuitions of Luigi Figini, who in his unequalled book *"L'elemento verde e l'abitazione"* (The Green Element and Living) imagined an ecological "transition" between architecture, nature and living. His house at the village of journalists in Milan, (also known as the "palafitta house", 1934-1935) is the declared manifesto of this, through its sequence of open-air rooms in search of a relationship between architecture and nature, climate, environment and context. Figini writes in the book, among other notes, "...the modern age is rising, and with the smoke of the first steam engine the city of stone becomes the city of concrete, of glass, of steel, and becomes more grey and gloomy, more inhuman. The last traces of the green element disappear, other new elements begin to dominate: smoke, dust, noise, miasmas; the vertigo, the chaos, the 'fever' of our time. The metamorphosis into city-barracks, city-prison has taken place" (Figini 1959).

It already reveals, therefore, the sickness of modern man, which architecture must oppose with its own means, a different idea of dwelling and living spaces, of relations, capable of relying on a humanising and not rigidly "machinic" relationship, opposing without doubt to the extreme figure of Le Corbusier's "machine pour habiter", an Italian-Mediterranean way, undoubtedly more poetic and sensitive to the landscape. "Where man, within the closed limit of a perimeter traced on the earth, superimposes room upon room along the vertical; where little land is no longer enough for a single family, but for many families, when man builds houses with many floors, and these houses are placed side by side to form a city, then the courtyard-historical patio, dies. In order not to die, it can only transform itself into its surrogate city: *the terrace-garden*" (Figini 1959).

But architecture and town planning always set new challenges, and Figini's poetics and his green dream were overlaid with *cities for nomads* on a planetary scale (the utopia between 1959 and 1974 of the Dutch artist and architect Constant Nieuwenhuys), as architectural megastructures dedicated to a new type of man and society. Or, at the opposite of the utilitarian society, it is the playful society as theorised by Johan Huizinga and developed by the Situationist International at the turn of the 1960s, in which man, freed from the automation of productive work, becomes capable of developing his own growth through play and creative development: discovering a mobile life as a perennial journey through the regions of the Earth, always in search of new stimuli and new possibilities for experience. In an environment where man's needs are already satisfied at the outset, aggression is sublimated and life becomes dynamic, in an architecture that has as its foundation the principle of 'disorientation', in favour of play, adventure, encounter and creative exchange.

New Babylon, as it was called, was thus born as *a concept of wandering*, from one part to another, in which man can finally build his own surroundings, regulating all material and climatic conditions and modifying its internal aspects. *A city that follows the course of paths*, constantly evolving and completely adjustable through mechanical devices. Basically, an idea almost sixty years old, not far removed from what happens today with our 'devices', as Branzi also writes.

New Babylon will remain a fertile idea for numerous re-elaborations and suggestions (the *Walking City* by Archigram, Lebbeus Woods, Yona Friedman among others), one of the most sophisticated and laborious examples of architectural megastructures, fundamental for its courageous audacity that anticipated Metabolism and the utopias of the 1970s, up to the recent theories of Rem Koolhaas. A nomadic utopia, Constant's, which, as history teaches us, ironically returns to relevance today, in our globalized world, and makes us reflect on a possible alter to our rational modernity, and the human isolation that has resulted from it (Ferrari 2015).

But it will be the challenge of the coming years for places, infrastructures, for living and moving on the planet even more surprising and full of innovation.

The theme of moving, connecting, living and ecological design, rethinking cities, living spaces, and infrastructures will be strongly conditioned by technology, by smartness, i.e. the ability to exploit artificial intelligence, devices to make better and faster use of our ways of moving, living and building new ecological landscapes.

All this obliges us today for the future to a series of even more articulated reflections, around space that changes, dilates and extends in its virtual, rather than physical, forms, and that refer to an image of infinity, of something that has no solution of continuity. Reflections capable of contributing to the transition from a polluted planet to a clean planet, playing the bet of the coming years on two determining factors: natural living and ecological movement. Almost like a return to a utopia, but concrete this time! (Scaglione 2015).

Mobile city

The rise of the metropolis had appeared as a dramatic, as well as contradictory moment of the modern age, to personalities like Antonio Sant'Elia, as well as to the other Futurists: the expanding city was the site of a complex interweaving of problems, from hygienic and functional to moral, political and cultural ones. A situation that forced the architects and town planners of Futurism, during the season of the first true modernity, the urgency of important changes to solve the most emerging problems, from viability to transport, from housing and domestic space, as well as the symbolic places of the new expanding city.

Outside Italy, almost at the same time as our futurist 'heroes', personalities of the calibre of Frank Lloyd Wright and Le Corbusier tackled the same themes in a courageous attempt to provide radical answers through evocative and extraordinary design scenarios, imagining the Ville Radieuse, the modern

06 | Le Corbusier, sketch for the town planning project of the Ville Radieuse

7 | A drawing appeared in an American magazine from the 1950s with the self-driving car.

city for three million inhabitants in the midst of trees, sunshine and widespread nature, and Broadacre City, the ideal American city founded on the single-family home, agriculture and urban gardens (which have now become one of the most widespread design ingredients!) and the automobile as an individual means of transport, as well as strange flying 'objects', already designed by Wright at the time, as suggestions for a technology that was friendly to nature and served mankind to improve its daily life on the planet.

As the Masters, it must be remembered that all the European neo-avant-gardes, as well as the American and Japanese ones, had bet their future design on the future of the city: a subject that remained a crucial protagonist of the debate and research that filled books and exhibitions from modernity until the 1970s. Up to the visionary ideas of the English Archigrams or our Archizooms, the former designing cities suspended on the ground or 'interrupted', cities in which the inhabitants could freely arrange their lives and in which moving, shifting, connecting, were crucial, the latter (together with Superstudio) proposing a tight critique without the city of capital, overturning its sense, structure and meanings.

Anyone who remembers Fritz Lang's 'Metropolis' (1926) will recall the dynamism of that idea of the metropolis, the traffic, the alienation, the 'machinations', as well as Ludwig Hilberseimer's disquieting urban perspectives, will have in mind those bright and quivering visions of a neurotic, flowing modern city, in which the machine, the infrastructure, were the nervous system of a new paroxysmal dimension of living. If that period has, to this day, shown its limits, despite its great innovative drive, it is time to turn the page: the ecological city is the only possible solution for the future, along with intelligent travel in a network of green corridors.

08 09 | Sketch and model of the New Babylon by Constant Nieuwenhuys (1959/74)

10 11 | Yona Friedman and his imaginary and utopian cities (1974)

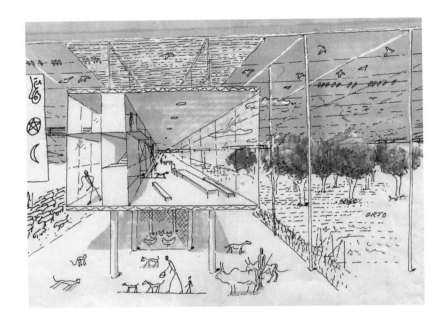

12 | Andrea Branzi, Agronica (1995)

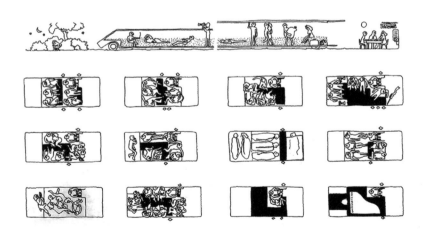

13 | Mario Bellini, design drawings of Karasutra, prototype house/mobile car (1972).

Mobile living

Far beyond emergency needs, research on the mobile home has been and remains a constant in many Italian and international experiences. The dwelling as a dynamic and evolving space, capable of allowing movement or expansion according to changing social or urban conditions, mobile for work or holiday, is again emerging as an important design topic. Temporary mobile structures, for events, initiatives, living and working, for tourism, whether seaside or mountain, which develop variable configurations and can be adapted to different needs, are again an object of interest for architecture and design.

Permanence and stability are today fleeting and uncertain terms in the accelerated whirlwind of the transformation processes of territories in the context of globalisation, but within the radical changes of contemporary society increased by technology, adaptability, flexibility, systemic versatility are emerging concepts and determining new conditions in the debate of the city, of places, of living.

Flexible and variable structures, temporariness and mobility, push future building within the paradigm of transience, towards design and construction solutions that can be transformed and adapted to dynamic conditions of use, with light, natural, recyclable materials, and in any case profoundly influenced by current and future mobility systems.

Houses and rooms, pavilions, services, public buildings, health facilities, are predisposed, with a new condition of flexibility and mobility of contexts, to respond to all those renewed needs that emerge, and will increasingly appear evident, from new ways and forms of living and from the impermanence and adaptability of contemporary living, played out between domesticity and neo-nomadism, also because "increasingly mobile phones and computers are determining domestic space" (Meschiari 2018).

And with the great exoduses of population, mobility, in its forms from the most extreme to the most consolidated, will expand the field of housing possibilities: welcoming refugees, exiles and migrants, true nomads and neo-nomads, the homeless, the displaced, the "free of spirit", young people in search of "love nests" and rooms/homes-parking, and all those new categories of contemporary society that appear destined to be housed, to mobile and temporary living, beyond the tradition of functions, to date, normally performed by the full range of permanent buildings that have produced irreversible transformations of our territories, cities, landscapes. The challenge is only just beginning, the role of Design, Architecture, Urban Planning, will be crucial if it is able to intercept, in the coming years, such impressive phenomena as this.

15 | Mario Bellini, Karasutra, prototype house/mobile car (1972).

16 | Lorenzo Papi, Studio Forte 63, Casa Albero (1972).

17 18 19 | Marco Zanuso, prototype of a temporary house (1970).

20 21 | Renault Symbioz, the car as an extension of the home, (2017); Symbioz predefines, according to Renault, the vision of the future of mobility with a 2030 horizon: this concept-car with autonomous, electric and connected concept car is a mobile extension of the house presented at the Frankfurt Motor Show in 2017. The design of the living space is by the Marchi Architectes studio.

From Noise to Silence, From Gray to Green
Mobility and landscape, a design experience within the infrastructure

The A22 is one of the main infrastructure pillars along the complex Brenner axis.

The traffic volumes (about 9 million transits to and from Austria, 52 million total accesses, 65% of which in the Alpine area) give back the dimension of a highly significant facility in the multi-scalar functionality of the territory, from the European threshold to the local one of the Trentino and South Tyrolean system, which pushes south to the Po Valley with its connection, at Modena, and the junction with the Autostrada del Sole motorway.

The motorway ribbon, in its Alpine part, constitutes an interface that organically innervates the backbone of the Adige and Isarco valleys and intersects a complex sequence of habitats marked by strong landscape specificities and interesting and progressive settlement dynamics. The motorway itself becomes a configuring element in terms of spatial quality, especially in consideration of a morphology that transforms the valley floor into a continuous proscenium with respect to the slope system, in an asymmetrical relationship: at the same time, in fact, the reading of the topography, conditioned by speed, gives the user of the infrastructure a partial view.

The A22 was and remains the first motorway to introduce photovoltaic noise barriers, to have hydrogen production stations, ecologically sensitive devices and equipment.

It is part of the infrastructure included in the Green Corridor (Modena-Munich) and has developed research and activities aimed at improving the future of mobility together with the future of living. Along the Munich-Modena Green Corridor, according to data from the Wuppertal Institute, it will be important in the next few years to install hydrogen production (at least 70 per cent equipment) and distribution centres (partly already completed, partly under construction), so that at least 15 per cent of hydrogen-powered cars can easily cross the Green Corridor.

The challenge of the years to come, for places, for infrastructures, for those who live and move on the planet, will be even more surprising and full of innovations.

The issue of moving, of connecting, of designing and rethinking infrastructures, roads, railways, metro lines and cable cars, will be strongly oriented by technology, by Smartness, that is, the ability to exploit artificial intelligence and devices to make better and faster use of our ways of moving.

All of this obliges us -nowadays for the future- to a series of even more articulated reflections, and which concern the role that planners, urban plan-

22 | Extract of the preliminary studies for the Autobrennero Green Corridor.
Research Coordinator Prof. Giuseppe Scaglione.

ners, technologists and engineers, designers, that vast array of protagonists of the world of reflection and design, of research and innovation, will have in the coming years, around the space that changes, dilates and extends in its virtual, rather than physical, forms, and that refer to an image of infinity, of something that has no solution of continuity.

In fact, it is - and will increasingly be - ecological and intelligent cars that are the new battleground of the mobile technology giants. And if until a few years ago these solutions were still an experiment, now they seem to be implementing a revolution that is about to involve and will incorporate in production and design, in the culture of moving, every type of vehicle, user, infrastructure.

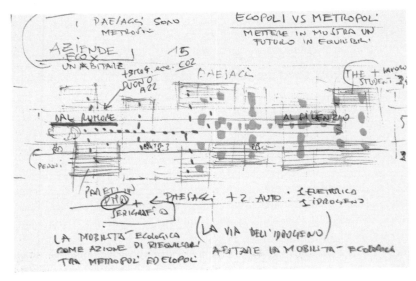

23 | Above_Green Mobility: Connected Autonomous Vehicles, source: www.eines.com/node/117
Below: Sketches for exhibition in Salone del Mobile di Milano, 2018, "From Noise to Silence, from Grey to Green".

From this research, as part of the partnership with Autobrennero, comes the project of the installation, placed in the courtyard of the State University of Milan, as part of the initiatives curated by the magazine Interni.

An Exhibit Design project, the result of a long research path, which set itself the objective of demonstrating that it is possible and necessary to re-construct ecological living, together with the need for intelligent infrastructures and mobility. The two themes, living-moving, are part of a single theoretical-design-social reflection, which in the next few years will increasingly concern the sustainable growth of living places, including open spaces and relations between people. It is a matter of imagining and designing the scenario of urban and domestic landscapes that may include - already in the coming years - a new energy transition, a more sophisticated aesthetics with a renewed focus on beauty, an ethics more humanly close to real needs and problem-solving, a different relationship with nature, and a significantly more effective and ecological metabolism.

On the basis of these premises, and of the cultural ones extensively described above, the installation project envisages placing two 'universes' in close confrontation: in a sequence of 'crossing' spaces, on the one hand, our current urban and life model is exposed: noise, pollution, congestion, traffic, oil-powered cars, living without quality, confused, disordered, energy-consuming, climatically unpredictable and with an inordinate production of waste. Showing also striking and real data of a dangerous, imminent debacle of the planet between global warming and crisis of seasons, nature, water and energy. In the sequence of the spaces following the starting path, in the second part of the installation, still in the path of the crossing, along the "corridor" that progressively turns from grey to green, the two sequences are "united" by the project. A new ethics, quality and beauty are the elements to take up the theme of the relationship with nature, along the sequence of "open-air rooms", taking the "green corridor", the final part of the exhibit route.

The direction is towards the dimension of living, moving and dwelling capable of guaranteeing a new ecological balance and a different quality of life. If the 'gray' side exposes the negatives of these last centuries of distorted modernisation, the 'green' side exposes data-ideas that show how we can change, reduce, improve. There is an explicit reference to the Encyclical 'Laudato sii' that Pope Francis recently launched precisely on ecology and respect for nature.

The sequence of pavilions, which make up the entire installation, were the subject of multi-handed design work in collaboration with of students from the course of Urban Design at UniTrento. "From Noise to Silence-From Grey to Green" represents the difficulties of today's everyday living and moving, and the proactive, welcoming, natural look of an ecological future.

In the different rooms, the "corridor", which unites them, fades from "grey" to green", the change in infrastructure and mobility in the coming years is represented, with the themes of living and moving from the present con-

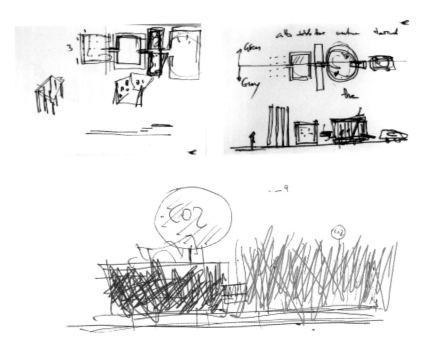

24 | Sketches for exhibition in Salone del Mobile di Milano, 2018, "From Noise to Silence, from Grey to Green"

Note: The summary, quotation or reproduction of excerpts or parts of a work, of images and their communication to the public are free if made for use of criticism or discussion, within the limits justified by these purposes and provided that they do not constitute competition to the use economics of the work; if made for teaching or scientific research purposes, the use must also take place for illustrative purposes and for non-commercial purposes.

dition towards a more ecological transition. The rooms, from closed become open, from anonymous become furnished and fitted out with eco-design objects and materials provided by partner companies.

The different pavilions have been designed with totally differentiated and differently perceptible external surfaces: from the dark grey of smog, towards a small green forest. Inside the crossing olfactory, sound, visual and tactile perceptions complete the narrative.

A scale reproduction of two cars in a single three-dimensional object (a traditional petrol/diesel car and an ultra-modern ecological energy car), bear witness to how the car is a paradigm of change in moving, living, not polluting, not making noise.

A meeting and relaxation area concludes the route, with the possibility of stopping, relaxing, discussing what has been seen and perceived, and hosting talks.

Bibliographic references

Branzi, Andrea. "*La città, Mobile*". In *Interni*, settembre 2018.

Drexler, Arthur and Paul Rudolph. *Museum of Modern Art*, 1970.

Ferrari, Marco. "New Babylon – L'utopia nomade di Constant". In *Artwort*, 2015. http://www.artwort.com/2015/06/23/architettura/new-babylon-lutopia-nomade-di-constant/ [accessed on 12/06/2021].

Figini, Luigi. *L'elemento verde e l'abitazione,* Domus, 1959. Ristampa anastatica, Libraccio editore, Milano, 2012.

Friedman, Yona, Kenneth Frampton, and María I. Rodríguez.*Arquitectura Con La Gente, Por La Gente, Para La Gente: Architecture with the People, by the People, for the People.* MUSAC, León, 2011.

Friedman, Yona. "Architecture Mobile", 1960, quoted in Ruth Eaton, *Ideal Cities: Utopianism and the (Un)built Environment,* London 2002

Friedman, Yona. "Mobile-Architecture. In *ArchEyes,* February 12, 2016, http://archeyes.com/yona-friedman/ [accessed on 12/06/2021].

Meschiari, Matteo. *Disabitare. Antropologie dello spazio domestico,* Meltemi, 2018.

#Process

The role of the University in co-designing the City

Marco Tubino

The research described in this volume is part of the actions undertaken within the framework of the Unicittà project, a programme of activities that is jointly defined and implemented on annual basis by the University and the Municipality of Trento, based on an agreement signed in 2016.

Like similar initiatives established in other European university cities, the Unicittà project stems from the shared desire to foster the integration and collaboration between two communities, the city and the university. It is aimed at promoting good practices of interaction, stimulating the academic community to propose activities that may generate opportunities for the city, encourage innovation processes, reorganization of services to citizens and satisfaction levels evaluation, propose new paradigms and tools to support government policies and practices and, finally, identify effective ways of communicating and involving citizens. The project pays specific attention to the investment in human capital and the enhancement of the skills of students who are trained at the University of Trento, promoting their involvement from planning to implementation of activities.

In this space of dialogue between the University and its city, the idea was born to involve the Department of Civil, Environmental and Mechanical Engineering in a path of accompanying the review process of the PRG. The University has taken the city of Trento, its environmental conditions, urban dynamics and ongoing transformation processes, as a case study to be addressed with a series of surveys and research actions, which have mainly pursued the objective of formalizing original and innovative theoretical hypotheses regarding the new paradigms of change in the contemporary western city, while accounting for the extremely delicate balance between the city and its immediate rural neighborhood.

The outcome of this scientific itinerary, which lasted five years, was the development of various elements of innovation in land governance that supported the municipal administration in the review process of PRG. However, back to the spirit of Unicittà project, the most significant result was the construction of a shared framework of objectives and vision of the future of a city that is undergoing a phase of profound transformation, of which the University itself is one of the most important drivers.

Founded just over sixty years ago, the University of Trento has profoundly changed the profile of the city and its region, favoring its economic and social development and cultural growth, as well as increasing its international visibility and accelerating the transition to a multicultural society. At the same time, its presence in the city has determined (and determines) opportunities and

01 | Adige River in the Rotaliana valley

critical issues, whose identification and composition emerge as central themes in the reflection on the future of the city.

In summary, these issues can be translated into the challenge of building a welcoming and attractive urban-territorial ecosystem, which is perceived by those born in there and those who come there to train or develop research as a suitable place to envisage and realize their project for the future.

The establishment of a university community, which is more than half made up by "foreigners", has implied new and wider demands for quality services (residential, mobility and sociality) and cultural offer, and has therefore determined the search and animation of new urban spaces, while promoting the contamination. On the other hand, the university community perceives its city and territory as a sort of natural "laboratory", from which it draws inspiration for research themes and curricula, and where it first experiments research insights and results.

Focusing on these issues and proposing or supporting creative actions is the mission of Unicittà, a project at the crossroad between a City that increasingly aims to innovate government practices and qualify services to citizens and a University that continuously grows, in size, expertise, outlook and needs. From these premises branch off the five challenges, or key-words, that also set the initial scene of the research that is presented in this volume: sustainability, hospitality, accessibility, innovation and beauty.

LEAF PLAN
TOWARDS THE ECOLOGICAL TRANSITION

Published by
Actar Publishers, New York, Barcelona
www.actar.com

Authors
Mosè Ricci & Sara Favargiotti

Edited by
Matteo Aimini & Sara Favargiotti

Graphic Design
Giulia Zantadeschi - Actar D

With contributions by
Mosè Ricci
Sara Farvargiotti
Bruno Zanon
Matteo Aimini
Davide Geneletti
Chiara Cortinovis
Francesca Marzetti
Silvia Mannocci
Anna Codemo
Giuseppe (Pino) Scaglione
Marco Tubino

Printing and binding
Arlequin SL

All rights reserved
© edition: Actar Publishers
© texts: Their Authors
© design, drawings, illustrations, and
photographs: Their Authors

This work is subject to copyright. All rights
are reserved, on all or part of the material,
specifically translation rights, reprinting, reuse of illustrations, recitation, broadcasting,
reproduction on microfilm or other media,
and storage in databases. For use of any kind,
permission of the copyright owner must
be obtained.

Distribution
Actar D, Inc. New York, Barcelona.

New York
440 Park Avenue South, 17th Floor
New York, NY 10016, USA
T +1 2129662207
salesnewyork@actar-d.com

Barcelona
Roca i Batlle 2
08023 Barcelona, Spain
T +34 933 282 183
eurosales@actar-d.com

Indexing
English ISBN: 978-1-63840-068-4
Library of Congress Control Number:
2022945930

Printed in Spain

Publication date: September 2023

The publisher has made every effort to contact
and acknowledge copyrights of the owners. If
there are instances where proper credit is not
given, we suggest that the owners of such rights
contact the publisher which will make necessary
changes in subsequent editions.